On the Case in the English Language Arts Classroom

On the Case in the English Language Arts Classroom

Situations for the Teaching of English

Thomas M. McCann
Northern Illinois University

Elizabeth A. Kahn
Northern Illinois University

Sarah Hochstetler
Illinois State University

Dianne Chambers
Elmhurst University

NCTE

National Council of Teachers of English
340 N. Neil St., Suite #104, Champaign, Illinois 61820
www.ncte.org

This book includes revised material that originally appeared in *In Case You Teach English: An Interactive Casebook for Prospective and Practicing Teachers* by Thomas M. McCann and Larry R. Johannessen, published by Pearson Education Inc.

Staff Editor: Bonny Graham
Interior Design: Jenny Jensen Greenleaf
Cover Design: Pat Mayer
Cover Image: iStock.com/sonia.ai

NCTE Stock Number: 34214; eStock Number: 34238
ISBN 978-0-8141-3421-4; eISBN 978-0-8141-3423-8

Library of Congress Cataloging-in-Publication Data

Names: McCann, Thomas M., author. | Kahn, Elizabeth A., author. | Hochstetler, Sarah, author. | Chambers, Dianne, 1950- author.
Title: On the case in the English language arts classroom : situations for the teaching of English / Thomas M. McCann, Elizabeth A. Kahn, Sarah Hochstetler, Dianne Chambers.
Description: Champaign, Illinois : National Council of Teachers of English, 2021. | Includes bibliographical references and index. | Summary: "Offers case studies in the teaching of English that prompt extensive discussion and written responses to problems that commonly confront English language arts teachers in middle and high schools"—Provided by publisher.
Identifiers: LCCN 2021034897 (print) | LCCN 2021034898 (ebook) | ISBN 9780814134214 (trade paperback) | ISBN 9780814134238 (adobe pdf)
Subjects: LCSH: English language—Study and teaching (Secondary) | Language arts (Secondary)
Classification: LCC LB1631 .M276 2021 (print) | LCC LB1631 (ebook) | DDC 808/.0420712—dc23
LC record available at https://lccn.loc.gov/2021034897
LC ebook record available at https://lccn.loc.gov/2021034898

Contents

Foreword

Peter Smagorinsky, *The University of Georgia, Emeritus*
Universidad de Guadalajara, Distinguished Visiting Scholar

I start every day with an online reading of three newspapers. The headlines tell a variety of stories about our turbulent world: wars here, shootings there, floods over yonder, fires on the horizon, politicians pointing fingers, and other events of the day. As one who has spent most of his life teaching and learning, I am especially attentive to stories about schools. Few of these stories are of the feel-good sort. Many involve errors of judgment committed by teachers who are confronted with situations where there are no good, easy, or obvious solutions. Many stories of this sort don't end well.

Early in 2021, a group of teachers in bucolic-sounding Sun Prairie, Wisconsin, was suspended for posting an online assignment in which students were presented with the following prompt: "A slave stands before you. This slave has disrespected his master by telling him 'You are not my master!' How will you punish this slave?" The lesson provided an additional piece of information: "According to Hammurabi's Code: put to death."

According to a news report on the incident, when a parent contacted one of the teachers, "the teacher said she didn't know it would be offensive and thought it would be a good discussion for the students to have" (Perez & Langrehr, 2021). Perhaps they should have thought that one through a little more. The main discussion following the assignment concerned how long the teachers would be suspended, and if they'd ever be invited back.

Teachers face all sorts of situations that a university teacher education program could never fully prepare them for. Programs tend to have one to two semesters of coursework, followed by student teaching. These courses are often designed with state certification rules in mind, and their content may be subject to political manipulation. In my state of Georgia, politicians with no experience as educators have moved to ban and even punish the teaching of critical race theory (which is not taught); diversity, equity, and inclusion (huh?); and social-emotional learning (which makes me mad).

Program space is tight, and teaching methods tend to displace other considerations. Yet on the job, teachers face any number of situations that require their judgment beyond whether to use small groups or not. Even life off the job can be precarious, as one teacher in a neighboring county of mine found when she lost her job after posting a photo of herself with a glass of wine in Europe on a summer vacation and locating it on her social media site where it was viewable by invitation only. Some people believe they learned everything they need to know in kindergarten. For the rest of us, learning never stops, and learning about teaching is a lifelong undertaking.

Which brings me to *On the Case in the English Language Arts Classroom*. The title is slightly misleading in that the cases include situations that extend well beyond the classroom, such as engaging with parents and administrators about controversial choices (not, fortunately, about how we would treat our obstreperous "slaves"), dealing with exhaustion from the workload and secondary trauma from students' complicated lives, developing appropriate relationships with students in extracurricular activities, and other relational and judgmental issues that teachers continually face, whether in classrooms or elsewhere. When I began teaching, I was much better prepared as a technician than as a social and moral figure on a school faculty. I learned about as much as I possibly could in my program at the University of Chicago and still came up well short in the range of understandings I needed to be a fully functioning teacher and colleague. I had to learn most of that through experience, and some of my lessons were costly.

On the Case in the English Language Arts Classroom, of course, goes beyond managing political and relational life outside the classroom. The dilemmas faced by teachers instructionally can bedevil the best of us. How does a teacher assign a controversial text in a school governed by conservative leaders who believe that teaching about racial discrimination is political and divisive and that not teaching about it is neutral and academic? What should a teacher do when an open-ended assignment about personal experiences produces writing that indicates dangerous behavior? How do teachers confront students and their parents over suspicions of cheating?

The authors classify such issues as "ill-defined" problems, those whose content is complex and whose solutions are difficult and perhaps impossible. The ones they present in this volume are mighty gnarly. Even as long as I've been in the business, I'd struggle with most of them myself. I think exploring these cases would greatly benefit beginning teachers—the primary audience for this book—whose teacher education programs provide good preparation for clearly defined problems such as how to produce bellringers and align instruction with standards. They often are not, however, prepared for what happens when instruction meets the fragile lives of students and becomes ensnared in the many contexts that impinge on teachers' judgment throughout the school day, week, and year.

The cases developed for this book may not cover the range of dilemmas that teachers will face, but they are representative of many types that will inevitably complicate teachers' lives and leave them staring at the ceiling at 3 a.m. It's possible that some of the predicaments depicted in these cases, or perhaps many of them, will occur just about every week of the school year. It's also possible that how teachers manage them will determine whether they keep their jobs. It's essential, then, that they have some experience in thinking about them and how they would handle them.

Hypothetical dilemmas have provided the foundation for discussions of moral reasoning, legal snarls, and many other areas. I took a course called Cases in School Administration from Dan Lortie during my doctoral program in which we analyzed problematic cases, an experience that confirmed for me that I never want to be a school principal. The cases in *On the Case* are well crafted and road tested for their verisimilitude and potential for provoking discussions of conflicts that have no obvious solution. There is value in exploring them, disagreeing about what to do, formulating provisional action plans, and considering the broader questions they imply. The point is not to generate a firm problem-solving road map, but to begin a process of becoming informed about the range of teaching responsibilities and challenges. In spite of the common belief that "closing the classroom door" will shut out problems, that door is always wide open, and people are watching. And when they don't like what they see, they will do what they can to stomp it out.

Deliberating about these cases allows early career teachers to begin generating possible solutions. As any experienced teacher knows, the same problem plays out differently with different sets of students, parents, colleagues, administrators, and other stakeholders. A single solution path is not possible to any ill-structured problem. What this case book does is enable teachers to begin the process of recognizing situations, reading contexts, anticipating responses, and formulating actions that require continual monitoring and evaluation. Perhaps classroom observations and student teaching will provide incidents that make the cases come alive for them. It's important for them to understand that these experiences are not definitive. Taking one teacher's solution with one group of students and applying it to new classrooms may produce disastrous consequences. That's some valuable knowledge to gain early in a teaching career.

The authors of this volume are outstanding teachers with an unusual knack for creating scenarios that produce worthwhile discussions. I anticipate that discussions of these cases will be provocative for beginning teachers and fascinating for teacher educators to run with their teacher candidates. I am a fan of the authors and their work in general and think that this volume will serve an important role in the social, political, and instructional development of the teachers fortunate enough to wrestle with the dilemmas that Tom McCann, Betsy Kahn, Sarah Hochstetler, and Dianne Chambers—under the watchful eye of our dear departed friend Larry Johannessen—have created.

Reference

Perez, J., & Langrehr, J. (2021, February 1). 'A grave error in judgment:' Sun Prairie teachers placed on administrative leave for virtual lesson. Channel 3000. https://www.channel3000.com/a-grave-error-in-judgment-sun-prairie-teachers-placed-on-administrative-leave-for-virtual-lesson/

Acknowledgments

Larry Johannessen was the coauthor of the first edition of this book. Anyone who knew Larry is likely to recognize his voice and spirit in some of the cases in this revised edition. After teaching for several years in high school, Larry devoted his work at the university to the preparation of teachers, and he cared deeply that early career teachers would thrive in their efforts to engage adolescents in the study of English language arts. We are indebted to Larry, not only for his direct contributions to this book, but also for his cherished friendship and his broader influence on our work and on the work of teachers across the country.

For many years, we have engaged preservice and veteran teachers in discussions about the cases collected in this book. Our university colleagues who have relied on the cases for their classes have shared with us their insights into the elements of the cases that students found particularly compelling and where the cases needed to be updated and refined. For their many collaborations and wisdom, we are particularly indebted to Judith Pokorny, Laura Bird, John V. Knapp, and Beth McFarland-Wilson.

We are especially grateful to our many university students who have discussed and written about the cases. We have identified some of these students by name in the last chapter of the book, but these are only a few of the hundreds of our students who have worked with the cases. These students have offered unexpected ways for responding to some cases and have advised us where we needed to clarify the narratives and the directions and where we needed to check the assumptions the narratives implied. Our thanks, in particular, go to the students in multiple sections of Sarah's ENG 194 classes at Illinois State University. These students reviewed cases and provided insightful critical commentary that guided some revisions to the book.

We thank Kurt Austin and the editorial staff at NCTE. Kurt has encouraged us and has patiently moved this project forward during a period of economic distress and social upheaval. We appreciate that he has recognized value in a case book that offers the potential to immerse teachers at all periods of their careers in deliberations about consequential instructional and organizational issues. We are indebted to Bonny Graham and her NCTE colleagues who have taken great care to prepare a book that we judge to be attractive and user-friendly.

I

Looking Forward

Planning for Case Study Discussions

For the first edition of this collection of problem-based cases (*In Case You Teach English,* 2002), Larry Johannessen and Tom McCann began by reflecting on their own experiences as high school English teachers and supervisors of teachers in order to construct the narratives about the kinds of problems that might cause teachers distress and might even lead to some solid teachers abandoning the profession. As Johannessen and McCann listed the possible cases, they quickly realized that they needed to consult with early career teachers about the episodes in teaching that caused them the greatest concern. This relatively informal investigation led to a more formal program of research about the concerns of early career teachers and their means for coping with difficult situations (McCann et al., 2005; McCann & Kahn, 2017). For this substantially revised and updated version of the collection of cases, we have drawn from this research and from our combined decades of preparing, supervising, and mentoring teachers. Although Larry Johannessen is not listed on the cover as one of the authors of this book, he has made substantial contributions to the effort, and we can recognize his voice and his spirit throughout the book.

Our hope with this collection is that the inquiry demonstrated in these cases will, in a sense, compress experience and equip teachers with the analytical and strategic procedures that will serve them well when the inevitable challenges and crises occur in their own teaching lives. We expect that the users of this book will experience the following benefits: the ability to

- anticipate a variety of instructional, organizational, and personal challenges that accompany the teaching of English
- generate and evaluate a variety of responses to common problems, such as censorship demands, plagiarism, classroom management, assessment anomalies, fatigue, rapport with parents and colleagues
- develop procedures for anticipating and avoiding problems and for choosing an appropriate course of action to respond to specific challenges as they occur

- cultivate procedures and dispositions for collaborating with colleagues and other stakeholders to find constructive, student-centered responses to problems
- recognize the conditions and positions that invite problems so that a teacher can avoid unnecessary risks and develop practices that support professional growth and student learning and satisfaction

A reflective person will gain knowledge and understanding from experience. Anyone who has experienced a troublesome situation might be able, in retrospect, to identify alternative courses of action or to weigh the true gravity of a problem. Although there is no substitute for experience, when it is possible to simulate an experience realistically, the actual experience might seem less threatening and practitioners learn some problem-solving strategies they can apply to new challenges. This is the expectation that guides the use of flight simulators for pilots in training and the use of automobile simulators for novice drivers. The same sort of thinking invites active learners to engage with others in analyzing problems and discussing the possibilities for action. Case study analysis is a common practice in graduate business schools, in law schools, and in leadership education. Both early career and experienced teachers can gain much through the process of deliberating about how to work through difficult situations. Every tough situation that teachers endure prepares them to deal constructively with similar encounters.

This text offers twenty cases for study and discussion. The cases introduce a variety of problem-based situations that very easily could confront an English teacher during the course of a career. Each case has the following characteristics:

- *Immediacy*: The case suggests some urgency to decide and act, so there is limited time to ponder, research, discuss, and select a course of action.
- *Action*: The case prompts discussants to deliberate and take specific action. The situation invites collaboration and emphasizes the value of consultation with others.
- *Detail*: The case provides sufficient description of the complicating factors and competing perspectives.
- *Problem*: Each case poses a challenge of such difficulty that it is not easy to find a simple solution and a completely satisfying response. Perhaps the best a person could hope for in each situation is to find the best course of action among some poor possibilities.

Recognizing That Bad Things Sometimes Happen

The following collection of cases might give one the impression that the teaching of English is a prolonged nightmare, with each day presenting new and harrowing challenges. On the contrary, we expect that a career in the teaching of English will be richly rewarding, and most days in the classroom will be pleasant. The cases presented here represent problem situations that we have experienced, or can imagine experiencing, over a twenty-five-year career. With our selected cases, we tell twenty brief stories. If someone teaches for twenty-five years and experiences all of these problem situations, that is a rate of less than one problem per year. If you faced all of these challenges over the course of a career, that would mean fewer than one potential sleepless night each year. However, if teachers are not prepared for challenges and assume that the world of teaching is a genteel, tranquil place, with no controversy and little animosity, they may very well experience nightmares or career-ending decisions.

Becoming a Reflective Practitioner

Cooper and McNergney (1995) argue that case studies help students of teaching to think like teachers because work with the cases provides preservice teachers with practice; they are "opportunities to encounter real teaching problems in the safety and security of simulated situations" (p. 5) where teachers can try out principles of teaching and learning without causing any harm to themselves or others in the process. Drawing on experiences in other fields and some work in education, Merseth (1991) maintains there are several benefits to be derived from applying case methods to teacher education programs. Cooper and McNergney (1995, pp. 5–6) reiterate these benefits, which we summarize here:

1. In deliberating about problem-based situations, participants immerse themselves in procedures for analysis and critical decision making.
2. The deliberations about the cases require attention to competing perspectives and multiple options, which promotes a reflective stance, in the spirit of Donald Schön's vision of "reflection in action."
3. As with any simulated experience, the work with the cases places participants in an imagined environment, with all of its nuances and complications, and requires decision-makers to operate within the rules of the environment.

4. Whether reflecting on the cases individually or tackling them as shared inquiry with peers, preservice or experienced teachers become actively involved in learning procedures for contending with tough professional decision making.
5. Group involvement with the cases prompts lively and extensive discussions that affirm collaborative efforts and promote a sense of community.

There is little research on the use of case method teaching in teacher education. However, Sykes and Bird (1992) and Grossman (1992), drawing on research by Spiro et al. (1987), conclude that case methods may be best suited for learning in areas that could be called "ill-structured domains." A key feature of such domains is ambiguity; they are domains in which relevant knowledge is not organized to fit a specific situation. As Grossman (1992) argues, "The value of cases for teacher education lies in their potential to represent the messy world of practice, to stimulate problem solving in a realm in which neither the problem nor the solution is clear" (p. 237). Teaching is an "ill-structured domain," and English teaching might be the most ill-structured or messiest of them all. Each day of English teaching, events unfold differently, and teachers must orchestrate a dizzying array of factors to encourage learning. Spiro and his colleagues (1988) argue that just learning general principles is not enough to help students learn how to operate effectively in "ill-structured domains," but the "structured dynamics of cases" are key to helping students learn how to apply the principles, or how to "reason from precedent cases" in such domains; the cases are absolutely necessary because they are the examples of the "abstract principles" (p. 379).

One of the most compelling arguments for using cases to prepare teachers, especially English teachers, is that they relate good stories. Cooper and McNergney (1995) state: "Stories are powerful and easier to remember than decontextualized information, and they seem to 'fit' with teachers' ways of organizing their knowledge of teaching" (p. 5). If this is true for teachers in general, then it is particularly true for English teachers. Stories are our stock in trade. We hope that these case narratives help developing teachers learn how to use important principles in their teaching and to become more reflective practitioners. Furthermore, as McNergney et al. (1999) argue in their collection of cases, deliberation about cases moves participants away from a conception of problem solving as isolated effort toward becoming a community of thinkers trying to advance an agenda to support learners. The collaborative effort is essentially democratic: "We believe that the main values of cases is that they enable individuals to connect with one another by focusing on common issues. In doing so, people learn about each other—another important benefit" (p. 13).

Selection of Cases

In selecting and developing cases, we have relied on memories of our own and others' experiences and the witnessing of daily crises to generate a list of case topics. To narrow our choices, we have relied on research about teacher concerns. Our own research (McCann et al., 2005; McCann & Kahn, 2017) reveals that beginning teachers have serious concerns about managing classrooms, about being viewed as credible professionals by their colleagues and by parents, about being liked and accepted by students, and about being evaluated by supervisors. We know also from our own experience with general methods courses and English methods courses that preservice teachers worry about how they will grade students, how they will respond to challenges about grades, and how they will handle a monumental workload. Preservice teachers also commonly express concerns about having the freedom to put into practice the concepts and beliefs about teaching they have embraced during their college or university preparation for teaching. We expect that the case studies we have selected will allow beginning teachers to face their apprehensions and to work with others to arrive at some strategies to make the prospect of problems less intimidating.

Although the cases have been created with preservice teachers in mind, they are also a resource that can be used in mentoring early career teachers, as we have discovered in using the cases as part of professional development programs in school districts. Moreover, even the experienced practicing teachers in our graduate classes have found discussions of the cases to be valuable by encouraging them to reflect critically about their own assumptions, principles, and practices. They often describe similar situations they have faced, and their contributions tend to lead to further discussion and reflection among participants.

We have provided a variety of cases: from logistical difficulties to moral dilemmas. We have tried to avoid both the mundane and the sensational. We are left with the fairly complicated cases that a teacher could face every year. We invite readers to examine and discuss cases that present problems worth discussing—worth discussing in the sense that a teacher could benefit from thinking through the conditions and ramifications with other reasonable persons. We expect that practice with some of the cases will help teachers develop strategies and habits of thinking that will serve them in times of crisis, so that challenges remain challenges and don't become nightmares.

Audience for This Book

The discussion and reflection about the cases in this text will support all English teachers, whether they have twenty years of experience or six months. These cases fit naturally into undergraduate and graduate preservice and in-service English education curricula. In the real world of English teaching, teachers must be prepared to handle unanticipated situations, to adapt current knowledge to deal with new problems, and to learn radically new things. In other words, English teachers must be able to deal constructively with change. To prepare English teachers to act creatively and intelligently in the classroom, preservice and in-service courses, workshops, and programs must become clinical laboratories where real teaching situations are confronted, pondered, and acted upon. Participants must have the opportunity to bridge the gap between theory and practice.

To become thoughtful and creative problem solvers, participants need practice in analyzing problems, in asking important questions, in considering a variety of responses, in arguing for or against different solutions or possible courses of action, and in seeking more than one answer to a problem. To be successful, English teachers must constantly think through problems to arrive at appropriate solutions. Donald Schön (1983) notes that teaching is a profession that invites reflection-in-action. Cases help learners understand concepts by actually experiencing them, by figuring them out for themselves, by holding them in their hands, by grappling with their nuances and subtleties, by testing solutions in an environment that encourages diverse perspectives.

Our teaching experiences and primary interests lie in the teaching of English; consequently, we have developed cases that feature situations common to English teachers. Some cases raise issues that hold special interest for English teachers. Other cases represent experiences that could confront any teacher, no matter what grade or subject. We include a case and issues matrix (see Figure I.1) so that users of this text can select those cases that have relevance and currency for their particular course of study or professional development goals. As we have noted, our experience suggests that veteran teachers, as well as early career teachers, benefit from studying cases. Problems arise in schools all the time; the problems become crises when they take teachers by surprise and they are ill-equipped to think strategically about the problems. Problems that grow unchecked have the dangerous potential to absorb time and attention, distracting the teacher from the instructional program that brings the joys and energy to our profession.

Case	6–8 Classroom*	9–12 Classroom*	Teaching Literature	Teaching Composition	Teaching Language	Censorship Challenge	Plagiarism	Managing Workload	Classroom Management	Diversity and Empathy	Balancing Work and Life	Grading and Assessment	Teacher Evaluation	Professionalism and Ethics	Critical Thinking
1. Surprise! We've Come to Complain		√	√			√			√	√					
2. Pressure Cooker		√						√			√		√		
3. Killing the Invaders		√		√					√	√				√	
4. The Accu-Grade System		√								√		√		√	
5. Teaching to the Test	√			√									√	√	
6. It Can't Be This Difficult	√			√	√										√
7. Out of Control		√						√		√				√	
8. It's Just a Soccer Game		√							√					√	
9. First Observation		√											√	√	
10. Doing the Right Thing		√												√	
11. Copycat		√					√		√			√		√	
12. To Think or Not to Think			√												√
13. Call Me Irreplaceable	√										√		√	√	
14. Evening Reveries		√									√			√	
15. When Do They Do Grammar?	√				√										
16. Teaching English among Many Languages		√	√	√	√			√	√	√		√			
17. Teaching in the Aftermath of Trauma		√								√				√	
18. Can't They Already Read?		√	√												√
19. Teacher or Technician?		√	√	√	√								√	√	
20. Isn't This Getting "Too Political"?		√	√							√			√	√	√

*Although we have designated that some cases are set in either middle grades or high school, the issues the teachers in these narratives face are ones that will concern teachers in both middle school and high school settings.

FIGURE I.1. Case and issues matrix for *On the Case in the English Language Arts Classroom*.

Format and Procedures for the Cases

This text provides narratives and an analytical framework for twenty cases. Many of the cases raise policy issues; some offer procedural challenges. With all of these cases, conversation is an essential part of the process of working toward a resolution. It is worthwhile for any teacher to recognize that in education one functions as part of a community, and constructive solutions and policies derive from collaborative discourse.

Each case begins with a preview, which includes a summary and a series of focus questions. The case narrative and related artifacts follow. A format for discussion guides the deliberation. The discussion questions will vary with the specific needs and details of the particular case. The following examples represent the kinds of questions that will guide reflection and discussion:

- What are the central issues in the case? If there is a controversy, what are the competing sides and interests in the case?
- If the case poses a management problem, what are the particular constraints or specifications you must meet?
- If the case raises a policy question, identify the needs that must be met, or the harms that should be reduced or eliminated.
- For each possible course of action, identify the likely benefits and potential disadvantages.
- Consider how others might evaluate your actions, including the possible unintended messages and consequences.
- If applicable, identify short-term and long-term solutions to the problem. Be prepared to explain your plan in detail, as well as how the plan is likely to lead to its intended effects.
- What are the merits of each of the perspectives in the controversy?
- To what extent does the case represent a political problem? In what sense are various parties competing for limited resources?
- Can you characterize the case as a structural problem that demands the careful design of organizational structures or mechanisms? If so, how can routines or policies be adjusted to avoid problems in the future and to support learners and teachers?
- To what extent does the case require the management of symbols that can spark emotional responses?

In general, the deliberation about each case is a *comparative advantage analysis*. Since each case does not lend itself to finding a "correct answer," perhaps the best we can do is find the best course of action among the several options available. So the deliberation process involves noting the possible responses to the problem, evaluating the potential benefits and possible disadvantages, and identifying the course of action that will likely accrue the greatest benefits and fewest disadvantages.

In some instances, facilitators might want discussants to contribute to online forums. These forums might be necessary when teachers cannot meet together, face to face; such forums can also extend a conversation that began in a classroom or meeting room. For these forums, the questions and procedures described above still apply. It would be wise for a group to collaborate in setting the norms for discussion, and a facilitator will want to specify expectations for contributions and for connecting comments to previous contributions. Such online forums are especially useful when participants write about the cases. See the examples in the final chapter of the book.

Since discussants are likely to be reading the work of educational authorities, part of the discussion could include a consideration of what these authorities might have to say about the problems exposed in the cases. For example, how would Lev Vygotsky respond to a plagiarism episode or a classroom management problem? What might John Dewey or Paulo Freire advise a teacher to do when faced with an assessment anomaly or a censorship challenge? The idea is not to find the authority-endorsed solution, but to bring these other voices into the conversation to expand thinking about possibilities.

History of the Cases

Over several years, we have used the cases in this book with preservice and practicing teachers. After using each case, we have asked the discussion participants to evaluate the case as an instructional activity. These evaluations guided us in choosing which cases to keep using and how to refine them.

We know that the cases will generate lively discussions, but what is the value of such discussion? In response to one case, a student observed, "It opened my eyes to things that teachers really have to deal with." The users of the cases testify that the details of the cases and the discussions about them expose inexperienced teachers to many unanticipated but crucial issues, some that are seemingly mundane and pragmatic challenges, others that are moral and ethical dilemmas. Discussion participants have commonly pointed out that the deliberation about a case exposed them to some issues and potential problems they had previously been unaware of. One person reported: "I believe the thought that goes into the factors of the case study and the discussion among students afterward are both valuable to future teachers in helping them decide how they might handle similar situations." Participants expressed a belief that the thinking they applied to a current case could transfer to new situations: "It helps you to think about the type of problem solving you will constantly be doing as a teacher and plan for some of those issues."

Our experience in using the cases with prospective and practicing teachers suggests that the cases are powerful instruments for preparing teachers for future challenges and encouraging them to reflect on current practices.

Note to Facilitators

Deliberation about each case will be most productive if each participant initially studies the case independently. Introductory questions can guide the reading. The facilitator might find it useful to have participants discuss the case in pairs or in small groups. In this way, everyone contributes insights and suggestions. Another phase of the process involves a larger group of participants in discussion. The large-group discussion exposes multiple perspectives and a variety of possible actions.

In no instance do we offer the "correct" answer for the problems posed by a case. Involvement in the case prepares teachers to reflect on difficult issues. Instead of guiding discussion participants toward a "correct" answer, the facilitator guides them in refining analytical procedures. This means that the facilitator will ask discussants to explain, support, and project: Why does someone make a particular claim? What are the logical consequences connected to taking certain actions? Are there any exceptions to one's generalizations? Does a proposal stand up to tests under particular circumstances? Who would disagree? What are the merits and shortcomings of the opposing views?

Sometimes discussion will be frustrating because some issues are so elusive and contentious that they do not permit satisfying solutions. Also, as sometimes occurs on the job, deliberation can end abruptly when a situation requires immediate action. In the end, explorers of the cases should recognize that this text provides no answer key. Some discussants will find it frustrating that a recognizable correct answer eludes them, and when this happens it will be difficult for the facilitator to bring a discussion to closure. Instead of pursuing correct answers as an end product, discussion leaders should look for reasonable analyses and the expression of strategic plans for confronting similar situations in the future.

Typically, a person who facilitates discussion about a case study follows these practices: (a) Allow the discussion participants time to prepare to discuss the case. In their preparation, participants might find it productive to identify several possible courses of action, predict the likely result for each course of action, and weigh the benefits and disadvantages of each choice. (b) As the discussion begins and progresses, rely on frequent paraphrases of participants' remarks, while avoiding evaluative comments. The other participants are likely to provide the challenges and evaluative comments to prompt a discussant to develop thought further. (c) Invite other participants to evaluate the analysis of previous speakers. (d) Press participants to be logical by posing appropriate follow-up questions: Why do you say that? What does that mean? How does that information support your claim? (e) Recognize that time constraints will dictate the necessity to bring a discussion to closure. In the end, the facilitator looks for evidence that participants have thought critically and strategically, in the sense that they have entertained multiple ways of looking at the problem and have made evaluative judgments about the most reasonable, ethical, and efficacious course of action. The facilitator can then summarize the essence of the discussion and perhaps prompt a written response or further research and writing.

Post-discussion Products

There are two obvious possibilities for post-discussion products. Some groups who work with a case might choose to play out the drama of the situation. After some preparation, the participants engage in role-playing to see how the proposed solutions would work: for example, enact a meeting with a disgruntled parent; engage colleagues about a new approach to the teaching of reading. In some instances, the case will invite a written response. The specific case will suggest the form and audience for the writing. In either case, taking some action after the discussion extends understanding of the controversy and allows participants to project the likely consequences for their decisions. In addition, a group might find that a case simply introduces the core of a complex issue, and some preservice teachers might wish to research the issue further and share findings with colleagues. Throughout the book, we suggest such research directions.

Writing Your Own Cases

The twenty cases highlighted in this book cannot account for the many difficult and frustrating situations that could emerge in a school every year. The instructor and other discussion participants who use this book might discover that they would like to write a case of their own and present it to colleagues for examination and analysis. Experience tells us that a case that stimulates meaningful discussion and promotes analytical thinking will have some key features. The last chapter of the book identifies these important features as a framework for producing new cases that are not represented in the current text.

II

Cases

1

Surprise! We've Come to Complain

Preview: How should teachers respond to parents' challenges about the literature that teachers require their students to read? This case asks the reader to consider whether some challenges have any merit and legitimacy. Is it dangerous to allow a potential censor to have any influence? In the following case, a relatively inexperienced teacher faces parents' complaints about certain required reading. The teacher must prepare for a meeting with the parents and decide how to work with the student who might feel uncomfortable with the current reading.

Focus Questions: (1) What planning should the teacher do for a meeting with parents who are voicing a complaint about the selection of literature? (2) How should the teacher treat the complaint and respond to the parents and to the student?

The Case: Surprise! We've Come to Complain

Lauren Saplin arrived at school early one Monday morning during her second year of teaching so that she could finish some preparation before her first period class. She had intended to put books on the desks and prepare a simple presentation slide with the directions for an activity her students would be doing during the first period class. Lauren estimated that she would be able to complete her preparations and still have time to use the washroom before she had to teach two classes in a row. But approximately thirty minutes before the first period bell, when Lauren entered the main office of the school, the administrative assistant noted that two parents were waiting to speak to her. Lauren thought, "Oh, no! I hope I didn't forget an appointment with someone's parents."

Lauren approached in her usual courteous manner: "Can I help you?"

"Are you Ms. Saplin?" the man asked. "I'm Oliver Carstead, and this is my wife, Amelia. Our daughter Louise is in your English class. If you have a couple of minutes, we'd like to talk to you about the reading you have assigned for your class."

"My first period class meets soon," said Lauren, "but I can give you a few minutes now. Come on in." Fortunately, the administrative conference room was available, so they slipped in there to talk.

After Mr. and Mrs. Carstead sat down, they told Lauren emphatically that they objected to her selection of John Steinbeck's *Of Mice and Men* as assigned reading in a ninth-grade class. Mr. Carstead took the lead in describing his disgust at the inclusion of profanities in the book. He opened a copy of the text and pointed to such words and phrases as *bastard*, *crap*, and *son of a bitch*. He also expressed concern that his daughter was exposed to the use of the "Lord's name in vain." Mr. Carstead showed Lauren instances in the text where characters uttered as expletives the words *Jesus* and *God damn*. The parents agreed that the most objectionable language of all was the repeated use of a racial slur, and pointed to several appearances of a most disturbing word in the text. Mr. Carstead noted that his daughter Louise was the only African American student in the class, and he understood that it was Ms. Saplin's practice to read several passages from the novel aloud during her lessons. Mr. Carstead appeared to Lauren to be quite agitated when he described his concern that his daughter would be the object of curiosity, unwanted solicitude, or perhaps derision as the students read these offensive passages aloud in class. Mr. Carstead noted that he hadn't read the entire book, but claimed that representative pages told him the nature and quality of the entire text.

The parents agreed that the most objectionable language of all was the repeated use of a racial slur, and pointed to several appearances of a most disturbing word in the text.

Lauren explained that she had some flexibility in selecting material for her class and that she had selected *Of Mice and Men* because she believed that it taught students important lessons about friendship and alienation. She explained further that it was her hope that the reading and the discussing of the novel would serve as a tool to fight race prejudice and hatred.

The minutes ticked away until Lauren had to point out that her first period class was about to begin. Mr. and Mrs. Carstead noted, "We are by no means done with this matter. We want to know what you are going to do about exposing children to this offensive book, and we want to know what you are going to do in regard to our daughter."

The first period bell was about to ring when Lauren agreed to meet with the Carsteads after school the next day. Of course, it was a little difficult to concentrate on the lesson at hand after this encounter. A number of questions and considerations came to mind: How would she defend to the Carsteads her use of the novel in question and convince them that it has some merit as a literary work? Should she bring other people to the meeting or meet with the Carsteads alone? How should she treat Louise Carstead? Lauren recalled that Louise had commented in class that she had already completed the reading of the novel. In some sense, then, the Carsteads' challenge seemed too late, and there seemed to be nothing that Lauren could do now. If Lauren were to excuse Louise from any lessons related to the novel, the separation would surely call attention to the girl and make her feel more uncomfortable. If Louise were excused from the current lessons, what would she do while the other students worked with the novel? Lauren tried to remember how she had introduced the novel. She couldn't recall if she had warned the students about the language. How could she explain to the parents and her supervisors the fact that she had exposed students to profanities and to offensive racial slurs without warning them?

"We are by no means done with this matter. We want to know what you are going to do about exposing children to this offensive book, and we want to know what you are going to do in regard to our daughter."

If you were in Lauren Saplin's position, what would you do? What would you do when you saw Louise Carstead in your afternoon class? What would you do in preparation for tomorrow's meeting? What provisions or policy changes, if any, would you make in the future?

Questions for Discussion

1. If Lauren has made any errors in the selection of the text, in reading parts out loud in class, or in requiring that everyone read it, where is she at fault? If you think she is not at fault, how would you explain this to the parents?
2. Is there anything that Lauren can do to ease Louise's discomfort in the class? Should Lauren make any exceptions for Louise? Why?
3. How can Lauren justify requiring her students to read a book that contains profanities and racial slurs?
4. To what extent would it benefit Lauren to include other persons besides the Carsteads at their meeting? Should she involve other persons, whether or not they actually attend the meeting? Who would she involve, and why?

5. What do you expect will occur at the meeting? What do you think the parents want? What concessions, if any, do you think Lauren should be willing to make?
6. What would you recommend as Lauren's plan for the next twenty-four hours? What are the projected benefits and possible disadvantages of your plan?
7. In the long term, what would you recommend that Lauren do? What would be the benefits to this long-term plan? In the end, what disadvantages can you predict will result from your plan? How can you show that, on balance, your recommended course of action will probably result in more benefits than problems?

Related Research and Writing

Research one of the following topics and share your findings with your classmates or colleagues.

1. Consult publications from the National Council of Teachers of English (NCTE) or the American Library Association (ALA) to learn which books are most often challenged. What are the most common bases for the challenges? What help can NCTE and ALA provide for teachers and librarians who wish to include some of the challenged titles as part of the literature curriculum or the school collection?
2. Read about one case of a censorship challenge in a school in your area or in the area where you hope to work in the future. What was the nature of the challenge? How did the teacher or the school respond to the challenge? What were some of the emotional aspects of the case? What was the final outcome? What did the whole episode reveal about mistakes and reasonable policies?
3. From a list of commonly challenged books, identify one work that you might find yourself teaching in the future. Expect a challenge to your use of the book. What would be the likely arguments against your using the book? How would you respond to the challenges? What provisions could you make in your class and with the school administration so that any censorship challenge does not escalate into a large-scale controversy?

2

Pressure Cooker: Where Should We Devote Our Energies?

Preview: Casual observers of education mistakenly assume that teachers face a relatively easy task. Only the conscientious practitioners and observers recognize how exhausting teaching can be. In the following case, a young teacher can ease her burden by abdicating the coaching responsibilities that she finds the best part of her job. Many teachers, especially in the early years of their careers, face the challenge of balancing extracurricular activities with teaching duties. Any teaching position makes many demands on a teacher's resources and endurance. Each teacher must decide how to allocate their energies.

Focus Questions: As you study the following case, prepare to discuss these questions: (1) Should Sandi Demos continue with her coaching responsibilities? How have you arrived at your conclusion? (2) How can Sandi balance her various responsibilities without damaging her health or compromising instructional integrity?

The Case: Pressure Cooker: Where Should We Devote Our Energies?

When Sandi Demos was hired at the same school where she had completed her student teaching, it was like a dream come true. During Sandi's student teaching at Claussen Community High School, South, her cooperating teacher was Dorothy Deiter. Mrs. Deiter had been at the school for thirty-five years and served most of that time as the speech team coach. Dorothy Deiter, or Dottie as she was affectionately known, was a legendary speech coach. Her teams filled a school trophy case with awards, including nine first-place performances at state competition and three first-place finishes at the national finals.

When Sandi was student teaching, she also assisted Dottie with the speech team. Sandi chaperoned trips to tournaments, judged selected speech events, and actually did some coaching. Her experience with the speech team was the highlight of Sandi's student teaching. She felt that she got to know the students personally and saw some talents they seldom exhibited in the classroom. Sandi especially enjoyed her relationship with her mentor teacher. Dottie always managed to maintain a positive outlook, even under the most trying circumstances. She seemed to have boundless energy and could always find time to talk to Sandi, whether it was about a lesson or a personal family matter. To Sandi, Dottie seemed more like a kindly aunt or a personal friend than a supervisor. Dottie seemed to Sandi to be the ideal teacher.

When Sandi was selected to replace Dottie as both teacher and coach when Dottie retired, it was a proud moment. Dottie's recommendation carried significant influence in the choice of Sandi as a replacement, and Sandi only hoped that she could in some small measure live up to the standard set by her mentor. To Sandi, her appointment as teacher and speech team coach seemed almost too good to be true.

By November, however, the euphoria of last spring seemed a shadowy and distant memory. Sandi was feeling overwhelmed. The combination of planning lessons, grading papers, attending to endless management duties, participating in professional development activities, and coaching a speech team was incredibly taxing. Like everyone else at school, Sandi was hurried and fatigued. She no longer had time for regular exercise, she bolted her meals on the run, and she averaged about four hours of sleep each night.

By November, however, the euphoria of last spring seemed a shadowy and distant memory. Sandi was feeling overwhelmed.

On a typical day, Sandi arrived early at school to do some preparation, expedite paperwork, and meet with individual students. She taught five classes, which required three different preps. Like her colleagues, Sandi monitored the hallways during passing periods and for a portion of her prep period. Sandi met her speech team members after school until about six o'clock. In the evening, she spent three or four hours in preparation and in grading papers. Of course, most weekends in the fall were taken up with speech tournaments, which typically ran Friday evening and all day on Saturday.

The constant grind of teaching and coaching had a serious effect on Sandi's personal life. To her friends, she seemed sullen. When she excused herself from social occasions, they thought she was trying to avoid them. Her sister and her parents found her uncharacteristically short-tempered and negative. Sandi's longtime boyfriend, Stuart, expressed concern that Sandi had lost enthusiasm for going out and having fun. She even fell asleep twice on a date at the movie theater. The fatigue became especially alarming when Sandi dozed at the wheel and nearly ran the car off the road as she returned from school after a speech tournament.

By December, Sandi had serious doubts about herself. She wondered, "What is wrong with me that I can't keep up and manage things? Dottie always seemed to take matters in stride and have abundant energy. Maybe I'm just not cut out to be a teacher."

When she shared her doubts with her parents, her father advised, "Why don't you just give up the coaching? You can't burn the candle at both ends. Your *teaching* is your job. The speech team is *extra*." Sandi couldn't bear the thought of giving up the speech team. With the strong speech tradition at Claussen, her selection as coach gave her immediate status and respect in the school and in the community. Her team this year had experienced considerable success, and she enjoyed being with the team. In fact, the only real joy she got out of her teaching position was her coaching experiences. Sandi told her parents, "If I give up coaching, I might as well give up teaching."

When Sandi confided her feelings to Stuart, this was his response: "Do you have to be Super Teacher of the Year? You take yourself too seriously. Don't assign so many papers. Give the kids a couple of days to just read in class, or have them do other stuff that you don't have to grade. Or just show some videos."

One of the veteran teachers at Claussen recognized Sandi's decline and suggested this: "Listen, kid. Whenever you're not feeling your best, take a 'mental health day.' You've got plenty of sick days. Just take a day off. The world will go on without you. Why make yourself sick by stretching yourself to the limit?"

She was nontenured, in a probationary period of her employment. The district could easily release her without cause if she stopped coaching.

To complicate matters for Sandi, she worried about the financial loss she would suffer if she quit coaching. She was not getting rich as a speech coach, but every little bit helped. She knew she was attractive to the district because she could both coach and teach. She was nontenured, in a probationary period of her employment. The district could easily release her without cause if she stopped coaching, and of course Sandi worried about losing her job. Claussen was one of the more affluent schools in the area and offered a competitive salary schedule. She had recently purchased her first new car, and she was eager to keep up the payments.

Sandi pledged to take plenty of time during the school's winter break to get some rest and to reflect on her future. She had to decide, first of all, whether she was going to continue as speech team coach during the second semester, with a speech tournament season that ran until April. If she endured the current year, she had to decide if she would coach in the future. Sandi also had to decide whether she was cut out to be a teacher at all. Could she go on teaching without the satisfaction she earned from coaching? **When Sandi returns to school after her winter break, what should she do?**

Questions for Discussion

1. How reasonable is it to expect Sandi to give up her coaching responsibilities? If she gives up her coaching position, when should she resign? What are the respective positive and negative implications associated with the decision to resign?
2. Recall the advice that other people offer Sandi. What do they advise? Assess the merits of each person's advice. Would you support any of these advisors?
3. Presumably, Sandi has entered into a contract with the school district to coach a team. Must she honor that contract, no matter what? Would a school district likely oppose her attempts to withdraw from her contractual responsibilities?
4. Does coaching a speech team carry as much weight as coaching a high-profile athletic team like varsity football or basketball? If there are any distinctions, how would they affect Sandi's decisions?
5. To what extent might Sandi be putting too much pressure on herself? To what extent is it reasonable for a new teacher like Sandi to try to model herself after a highly respected veteran teacher? What are reasonable self-expectations for a new teacher?
6. How viable is it for Sandi to achieve a better work-life balance without sacrificing her standards? If Sandi were to achieve a healthier balance, what would this look like?
7. How vulnerable is Sandi to losing her job? Realistically, would a school district release a teacher because she honestly felt she could no longer coach? If this were the case, how could the teacher challenge the dismissal?
8. Devise a short-term and a long-term plan for Sandi. Through your analysis, show why your recommendations would be the best plan for Sandi.

Related Research and Writing

Research one of the following topics and share your findings with your classmates or colleagues.

1. Talk to personnel directors or department chairs in several schools in your area or where you hope to work to determine whether extracurricular responsibilities are a required part of a teacher's job. Are new teachers, especially, expected to take on a coaching or club supervision role? If extracurricular duties are part of the job description for a teacher, why does the school judge these duties to be an important part of the job?
2. Interview a teacher who is also a coach or club sponsor. How does the teacher handle the time-consuming extracurricular duties without allowing those responsibilities to interfere with the quality of their instruction?
3. Read some of the research about stress, school climate, and the effects these factors have on teacher morale. What are some of the dangers associated with the pressures teachers feel when their jobs demand long hours and confront them with various responsibilities? How do some veteran teachers manage the workload effectively? What strategies have teachers found to manage stress in a constructive and healthy way?

3 Killing the Invaders: Respect, Confidentiality, and Security

Preview: In the following case, a situation challenges a teacher's pledge to respect confidentiality. The teacher must decide if something more is at stake than his promise to keep students' writing confidential. In the process, the teacher must determine whether the ideas expressed in a student's writing constitute a genuine threat. At the same time, the teacher must determine whether he has to respect the right of each student to harbor any thought they wish, no matter how hateful or disturbing the teacher finds that thought.

Focus Questions: As you read the following case, prepare to discuss the following questions: (1) Is there a real and immediate threat to anyone? (2) Must the teacher keep his pledge to maintain confidentiality? (3) In the end, what immediate and long-term actions should the teacher take?

The Case: Killing the Invaders: Respect, Confidentiality, and Security

On Sunday evening, Rodney Welkins immersed himself in his usual routine of reading students' writer's logs from the previous week. He wasn't exactly *grading papers* in the usual sense. Rodney had students keep a writer's log in his Writers Workshop course as a means for collecting their thoughts and exploring ideas. Rodney gave students credit for this writing, but he felt that he couldn't grade the logs in the sense of *correcting* them or making evaluative judgments about their exploration of ideas. Instead, Rodney responded to the students and their writing in a personal way—by asking questions, sharing similar thoughts, and offering encouragement.

Rodney viewed the students' use of the writer's log and his responses to them as key elements in his approach to writing instruction. When he introduced the writer's log concept to his students, Rodney assured them that they could write anything they wanted, using whatever language and forms of written expression they desired. If the students' writing were to be genuine, honest, and fresh, insisted Rodney, the students must be free to choose topics and modes of writing they valued and that represented who they were. Rodney earnestly hoped to avoid channeling students' efforts into producing the predictable party-line drivel that was intended only to satisfy the teacher. In the spirit of this approach, Rodney had to honor a commitment to freedom and confidentiality: students must have the freedom to say whatever they wanted in their logs, and Rodney must respect the privacy of their thoughts by not sharing the students' writing with parents, colleagues, and school administrators without the writer's permission. In the past, some students had tested Rodney's resolve to allow freedom of expression and to keep their work confidential. Some students used vile profanities; some professed hatred of other teachers; and some recalled sexual exploits and experience with the use of controlled substances. In each case, Rodney made no judgments and respected what he saw as the private thoughts of the writer.

In the past, some students had tested Rodney's resolve to allow freedom of expression and to keep their work confidential.

As Rodney worked his way to the bottom of the stack of writer's logs, he opened one that he found particularly disturbing. The log belonged to Kyle Pattard, a reserved but generally cooperative eleventh-grade student. Kyle's log entry was apparently a response to a recent class discussion about persuasion and policy issues. The example the class explored was the government interdiction of refugees who attempted to enter the United States outside of the established border crossings. Here is what Kyle wrote:

> We don't need one more alien in our country. Their attempts to enter America illegally should be considered an invasion. The army or border agents should use whatever means they have to push back the invasion. I would like to be a border patrol agent. I'd be happy to pull the trigger on the people who attempt to enter illegally. It's like fighting against people trying to break into your home.

On the top of the page, Kyle had printed in large letters "KILL, KILL, KILL!" He also illustrated his entry by drawing a crude picture of someone pointing a gun at someone hiding behind a cactus (see Figure 3.1).

Rodney was stunned and disgusted when he came across this entry. His instinctive reaction was to write a long, critical response to Kyle, pointing out his failure to use reason, and urging him to abandon the hateful attitude represented by the log entry. Rodney hesitated to respond in this way, but he was concerned about the potential seriousness of Kyle's comments.

FIGURE 3.1. Kyle's writer's log entry.

Any threats of physical violence in schools have to be taken seriously. In the past year in the same state, there had been three cases of school shootings. During the fall semester, there was a bomb threat in a neighboring district, where police specialists had to remove a homemade pipe bomb from the girls' locker room. In each case, the perpetrator was a disaffected student who expressed rage against a target group in the school.

Any threats of physical violence in schools have to be taken seriously.

Kyle's writer's log entry triggered memories of some unfortunate episodes in class. Rodney recalled that Kyle commonly avoided the Latinx students in class. Whenever there was cooperative group work, Kyle discreetly asked not to be teamed with Latinx students. Rodney, of course, refused such requests, recognizing that a strength of cooperative learning is that students learn how to work with everyone. However, when Kyle was teamed with Latinx students, he remained silent, sitting with arms folded, contributing nothing to the group. Since Latinx students constituted approximately 30 percent of the school population, it was inevitable that most cooperative groups would include at least one Latinx student.

As Rodney read and reread Kyle's writer's log entry, he wondered how serious the threat was. He feared that there was an immediate concern because a significant portion of the school's enrollment was Latinx, most of whom were Mexican American. Rodney worried that Kyle might be capable of a violent attack, or that an overt expression of his hateful attitude might prompt a violent response. At the same time, none of Kyle's other writer's log entries had the same tone or expressed similar sentiments. Rodney wondered if perhaps he was overreacting.

Rodney knew that if the log entry even hinted at a child's suicidal tendencies, or if the entry expressed an overt threat to a particular student or teacher, he would have to share the student's writing with authorities who could intervene. In this case, however, Rodney felt that although he was disgusted with the ideas that Kyle expressed, he could not determine that Kyle posed a genuine threat targeting specific students in the school.

Rather than ponder the question alone, Rodney decided to phone Yolanda Beekers, a veteran science teacher whom the school district had assigned to him as a mentor. When Rodney reached her, Yolanda observed, "Maybe the boy is just trying to shock you. If he has not gotten into trouble before and hasn't posed a real threat in your class, maybe he is just exaggerating, the way adolescent boys will. I would talk to him, though; and I would show the writing to the assistant principal. I know you want to keep the writing confidential, but you also have to protect yourself."

"I know you want to keep the writing confidential, but you also have to protect yourself."

Yolanda was definite about what she thought Rodney should do, but he still felt uncomfortable about sharing the student's writing after promising that he would keep the logs confidential. Rodney felt that he would violate a promise and contradict the approach he was trying to take in the teaching of writing.

Rodney Welkins faces at least two major decisions: (1) What, if anything, should he write as a response in Kyle's log, or say to Kyle in a conference? (2) Should Rodney violate the promise of confidentiality by sharing Kyle's writer's log entry with other adults in school or with Kyle's parents, without Kyle's permission? **If you were in Rodney's situation, what would you do?**

Questions for Discussion

1. What are the possible courses of action Rodney might take? For each possible course of action, identify the likely benefits and potential disadvantages.
2. In this case, to what extent does Rodney have an obligation to keep his pledge of confidentiality? By what standard would you decide there is an obligation?
3. According to the information presented in this case, to what extent is Rodney under any legal obligation to report Kyle's written views to anyone?
4. In this case, what claims, if any, does Kyle have to the right to the privacy of his thoughts?
5. To what extent does Rodney have realistic and compelling concerns for the dignity and safety of Kyle's classmates?
6. If Rodney finds Kyle's written expression vile and dangerous, how responsible is he for trying to change Kyle's views?
7. How possible and practical is it for any teacher to make the kind of pledge of confidentiality that Rodney has made with his students?
8. Part of Rodney's dilemma stems from his approach to the teaching of writing. Comment on the merits of his approach and the assumptions he makes about how students develop as writers.
9. Identify short-term and long-term solutions to the problem. Be prepared to explain and defend your plan in detail.

Related Research and Writing

Research one of the following topics and share your findings with your classmates or colleagues.

1. Read the work of someone who is a proponent of using journal writing and freewriting as a means to develop writing skills and to discover an authentic voice for writing. Why does the proponent find it important for writers to use journals? How is freewriting intended to promote authentic voice? What problems could a teacher face when they rely on journal writing as an essential part of writing instruction?
2. Talk to personnel who have responsibility for security at a local school. To what extent do they judge their school to be a safe environment? What are their primary security concerns? What are they doing to provide a reason-

able guarantee of safety in the school? To what extent must a teacher be concerned about safety?

3. Read reports about the current state of safety and security in schools. How have schools changed in regard to security in the last ten years? Generally, have schools become safer places for children? What more could schools be doing to protect the safety of children?
4. Talk to a teacher in a local school. Find out what teachers are *required* to do when they read in students' writing issues about neglect, abuse, the potential for violent behavior, or the suggestion of suicide. What guidelines do teachers have for determining when a student is making a veiled threat or when the student is crying out for help? Report to your classmates or colleagues about what you learned about local policies.
5. Laws regarding the disclosure of students' writing to parents, school officials, and other authorities differ from state to state. For example, in some states, the law requires that if teachers obtain from students' writing information about possible child abuse or neglect, they must report that information to the proper authorities. Investigate the laws in your state regarding the kind of information, and under what circumstances, teachers are required to disclose to parents, school officials, or other authorities. How do the laws in your state relate to the kind of problem presented in this case?

4 The Accu-Grade System: What Is a Fair Grade?

Preview: Teachers commonly complain that grading is one of the worst aspects of their job. Not only is the task tedious, but the teacher inevitably faces some difficult and emotional decisions. As much as teachers try to make calculating scores as objective and accurate as possible with the use of gradebook software, some subjectivity will be necessary. In the following case, the teacher faces several awkward judgment calls. He knows that the numbers in his gradebook do not add up to his assessments of the students' capabilities. The teacher is left to ponder how to be fair to all of his students.

Focus Questions: As you read the case, keep the following questions in mind: (1) How would you calculate grades for the four students who are profiled? (2) How can the teacher determine a reasonable grade for each student? (3) How can the teacher be fair and consistent at the same time?

The Case: The Accu-Grade System: What Is a Fair Grade?

Jeremy Flanders dreaded making decisions about students' grades at the end of the semester. As he pondered his gradebook on this late evening in January, he faced the kind of assessment anomalies that seriously disturbed him. Jeremy had been using the district's gradebook application to record and calculate grades. He had hoped that the program would make his decisions easier and more objective: just enter the credit for tests and assignments and the grades are calculated. Jeremy could provide each student with a summary and say, "There you have it. The numbers don't lie." But inevitably, he had to make some subjective judgments without the assistance of the gradebook. The difficulty in making decisions about grades was apparent in the case of four of Jeremy's students. These students were in his "average ability" sophomore English class. Their grade profiles appear in Figure 4.1.

Accu-Grade
Summary Grade Report
Teacher: Flanders

Whitney Patel

Homework Assign	Tests/ Quizzes	Major Essays	Sem Exam	Sem Total	Semester Percent
200	278	140	75	693	75.3
200	350	200	170	920	100

Stephania Radzienski

Homework Assign	Tests/ Quizzes	Major Essays	Sem Exam	Sem Total	Semester Percent
200	88	112	106	506	55.0
200	350	200	170	920	100

Axel Wiscomb

Homework Assign	Tests/ Quizzes	Major Essays	Sem Exam	Sem Total	Semester Percent
170	225	135	85	615	66.8
200	350	200	170	920	100

Jamal Wicker

Homework Assign	Tests/ Quizzes	Major Essays	Sem Exam	Sem Total	Semester Percent
72	81	185	165	503	54.7
200	350	200	170	920	100

FIGURE 4.1. Accu-Grade summary report.

The four profiles were puzzling. First, an examination of Whitney Patel's numbers would indicate that she passes with a C, at 75.3 percent. Whitney is a student who attends class regularly and completes all her assignments. She passes mostly on the strength of her homework completion. She has also done reasonably well on the assignments that Jeremy has labeled "major essays," which means multiple-paragraph compositions she developed through a deliberate process over several days. For Jeremy, the troubling aspect of the grade profile was the fact that Whitney performed poorly on the semester exam (44 percent). The semester exam requires that students answer comprehension questions about the short texts they read on the day of the test, and that they write an essay. Presumably, the semester exam provides a measure of how well students can *independently* read and write. One would have to wonder, then, how it is possible to pass Whitney if she cannot demonstrate that she can read and write at a level of performance expected of tenth graders. Although Whitney completed all of her homework assignments, and she earned fairly good grades on her essays, these sources of assessment did not provide measures of independent work. In fact, sometimes Jeremy wondered if Whitney's parents had actually done most of her work for her. In the end, the only thing Jeremy could say with certainty was that Whitney Patel is a conscientious student who attends class every day and completes all of her homework. He could not say that Whitney could read and write the way students were expected to in tenth grade. Jeremy thought, "If I pass Whitney, it's basically because she's a nice kid who does all her work, and the computer tells me that I have a numerical basis for passing her."

Stephania posed another kind of problem. At 55 percent, the summary number indicates that she should fail the class. Jeremy had already followed the school policy by notifying parents when students were failing or near failing, so a failing grade would come as no surprise to any of his students having difficulties. Like Whitney, Stephania completed all of her homework, but she performed poorly on tests and quizzes. Many of the quizzes were basic recall questions intended to prompt students to keep up with their assigned reading. Stephania also had some difficulty with the major essays. At the same time, on the semester exam, a measure of a student's independent ability to read and write, Stephania earned a passing grade. In the end, Jeremy wondered, doesn't the semester exam in itself show that this student has achieved the goals of the course? The problem was further complicated because Jeremy knew that Stephania had Tourette's syndrome and was legally blind in one eye. Perhaps her ability to overcome these challenges makes her performance on the semester exam even stronger. But shouldn't she be held to the same performance standards as all the other students in tenth grade?

In the end, Jeremy wondered, doesn't the semester exam in itself show that this student has achieved the goals of the course?

If Jeremy felt uncomfortable in failing Stephania, he felt even worse about the prospect of passing Axel Wiscomb. Like Stephania, Axel had difficulty with the semester exam. In fact, he failed miserably, with a 50 percent score. If he relied on the semester exam alone, the teacher would have to say that Axel cannot read or write at the standard that could reasonably be expected of tenth graders. Consistently, Axel's essay grades were Ds. He barely scraped by on essays and tests when he was provided a lot of support in class. When he worked independently, he could not make a passing grade. Although Jeremy would not openly admit it, he would *like* to fail Axel. Axel's attendance was irregular and he often was tardy for class. Axel was often disruptive and occasionally disrespectful toward the teacher. In general, Jeremy thought that Axel had a bad attitude. Yet his grade was close to a C, according to Jeremy's scale. In truth, if Axel were a more pleasant and cooperative student, Jeremy would be tempted to round the score off to an even 70 percent. But Jeremy wanted to remain objective.

Although Jeremy would not openly admit it, he would like to fail Axel.

Perhaps the most distressing situation of all was Jamal's. His total score and percentage (54.7 percent) for the semester would indicate that he should fail. In fact, the total percent reveals that he is not close to passing. There isn't even the possibility to round the final percentage in his favor. He has turned in very little homework, and he has little accumulated credit on tests and quizzes because he has been absent frequently and never made up the tests he missed. At the same time, he has done remarkably well on the major essays. Jeremy remembers showing one of his colleagues Jamal's essay about *Dr. Jeckyll and Mr. Hyde*, and they both agreed that the essay was brilliant. Jeremy knew that Jamal had written the essays himself, because Jeremy had seen the early drafts as students worked on them in class. Jeremy was confident that Jamal's essays were reliable evidence of his considerable writing ability.

Jeremy had a lot of sympathy for Jamal. His father died when Jamal was very young. Now his mother is battling cancer, for which she receives regularly scheduled chemotherapy. The chemo treatment leaves Ms. Wicker weak and incapacitated. At these times, Jamal takes over responsibilities at home, causing him to be absent frequently.

There were several emotional reasons for Jeremy to recognize extenuating circumstances and pass Jamal. To complicate matters, Jamal was a top swimmer on the school's boys' varsity team. Jamal's failure in English could make him ineligible to compete, which would have a devastating impact on the team and deny Jamal one motivation for staying in school during a trying period in the Wicker family's life. At the same time, Jeremy had always carefully avoided showing favoritism toward star athletes. If Jeremy passed Jamal at 55 percent, he might as well pass everyone in the class.

If Jeremy passed Jamal at 55 percent, he might as well pass everyone in the class.

Jeremy knew that his principal, Dr. Flores, emphasized that teachers should text her at any time if they had a question about anything. He knew it would help to talk about his questions with someone more experienced, but he worried that it was too late to reach out, and he doubted that he had Dr. Flores's contact information in his phone anyway.

As Jeremy pondered his dilemma, he reminded himself that the goals for English focused on *literacy*, not on regular *attendance* or the *amount* of homework completed. Jeremy also told himself that he had a responsibility to the students and to his colleagues to be consistent, or else any assessment would be meaningless. As difficult as it was going to be, Jeremy would have to make decisions and turn in grades the next day. **What grades should he submit for these four students? How can he justify his decisions?**

Questions for Discussion

1. On what factors should Jeremy base his decisions about the grades for the four students? Is it possible to be absolutely objective? If one is justified in making some subjective judgments, where does that subjectivity end?
2. What are the dangers in making subjective, or even impressionistic, judgments about the assessment of students' academic performance?
3. Jeremy is in danger of letting emotion and sentiment influence his judgments about students' grades. To what extent do these *feelings* have an appropriate place in assigning grades?
4. To what extent should Jeremy take into account the potential reactions of his colleagues to any decision he might make about grades for his own students?
5. What do you think about Jeremy's *system* of grading? Are there any adjustments he might make to allow the system to support the grades he is inclined to make anyway? In a sense, would this adjustment be stacking the deck against some students and in favor of others?
6. How can Jeremy assign grades that will be consistent with his inclinations and allow him to justify his decisions as fair and accurate?
7. What are some potential problems with Jeremy's commitment to being "fair"? Should he consider that equality might be more favorable than equity?
8. Look at the language Jeremy uses around assessment: what are the potential effects of his framing around "giving" a student a grade rather than a student "earning" a grade?

Related Research and Writing

Research one of the following topics and share your findings with your classmates or colleagues.

1. Seek access to a common grading application, such as one used at your school, your clinical site, or a free one online, and spend some time interacting with and analyzing it. What assumptions do the software producers appear to make about student learning and assessment? What are the strengths of the program? What cautions would you offer someone who relies on such a program?
2. Talk to at least two veteran teachers about the process they use for grading. Do they use points or weighted assignments? What "counts" for the most and least in the calculation of a semester grade? After your conversation, devise your own process. Describe your process to your classmates or colleagues and provide a rationale for your method of calculating grades.
3. Interview three or four middle school or high school teachers about their approach to grading. To what extent do these teachers attempt to keep their judgments "objective" and guard against bias? Based on this small sample of experienced teachers, how much do teachers take into account a learner's personal challenges when determining a grade?

5

Teaching to the Test

Preview: Although teachers typically enjoy a great deal of autonomy in their own classrooms, no teacher has complete freedom. Various sources impose demands on a teacher. A beginning teacher will feel pressure to conform, even when conformity means compromising the instructional approaches that appear to have the greatest merit. How can a teacher maintain instructional integrity and also answer the demands of others? Is it realistic for a teacher to expect to teach the way they were prepared to teach as a student in a methods class?

Focus Questions: As you read the following case, prepare to discuss the following questions: (1) Must the teacher in this case follow an instructional plan that the school principal sponsors? How much autonomy does the teacher have to make the instructional decisions in her own classroom? (2) To what extent should mandated state assessments guide a teacher's instructional plans?

The Case: Teaching to the Test

When Esmeralda Huerta went to her faculty mailbox during the first week of February, she found a note from the principal's administrative assistant: "Please stop by the principal's office today to pick up your SAP material." Although Esmeralda was in her second year of teaching, it was her first teaching sixth grade and her first experience with administering SAP, the state-mandated writing assessment. She viewed the test as an imposition on her instructional time, but she recognized that it was a requirement all schools in her state were obliged to complete. Realistically, Esmeralda thought, she and her students could afford to sacrifice a couple of days of instruction in order to accommodate the writing test.

Esmeralda was surprised and more than a little annoyed when she picked up the test preparation materials and read the attached memo from the principal:

TO: Sixth-Grade Teachers
FROM: Eleanor Bobbins
DATE: January 27
SUBJECT: SAP Test Preparation

As I suggested at the beginning of the year, the six weeks before the State Assessment Program (SAP) tests will be devoted to preparing students to be successful on the exam. Remember that the students' performance on the tests is a reflection on our school and on your instruction. The attached booklets have been provided to assist you in preparing your students. You will follow the daily plan suggested in the booklets to train students for the exam. Please see me if you need more booklets or if you have any questions about their use.

When Esmeralda made her way to her classroom and examined some of the materials, she was crestfallen. In her judgment, the test preparation booklets intended for student use promoted formulaic writing and relied on simpleminded analogies. Essentially, the lessons in the booklet prompted students to use a rigid template to guide their production of compositions and structured practice with the state's scoring rubric for students to assess one another's papers.

In her judgment, the test preparation booklets intended for student use promoted formulaic writing and relied on simpleminded analogies.

One representative lesson directed students to think of the organization of their narrative as parts of a slice of pizza, with the supporting crust representing the overall focus and the toppings representing the descriptive details and expression of events (see Figure 5.1). The lessons for the persuasive writing sample encouraged students to follow the "triangulation approach," which directs the writer to conceive of any topic as having three aspects or components. Under this system, the writer would express a general claim that has three parts (see Figure 5.2). For example, the writer might respond to a question about holding school on Saturdays by claiming, "We should not have classes on Saturday because children need time to relax, teachers need time to prepare, and custodians need time to clean and repair the school building." In the body of the composition, the writer would develop each of these three reasons and provide explicit transitions.

The lessons prescribed by the test preparation booklets were diametrically opposed to the kind of writing instruction Esmerelda understood to be the most honest, effective, and worthwhile. The rigid and prescriptive nature of these

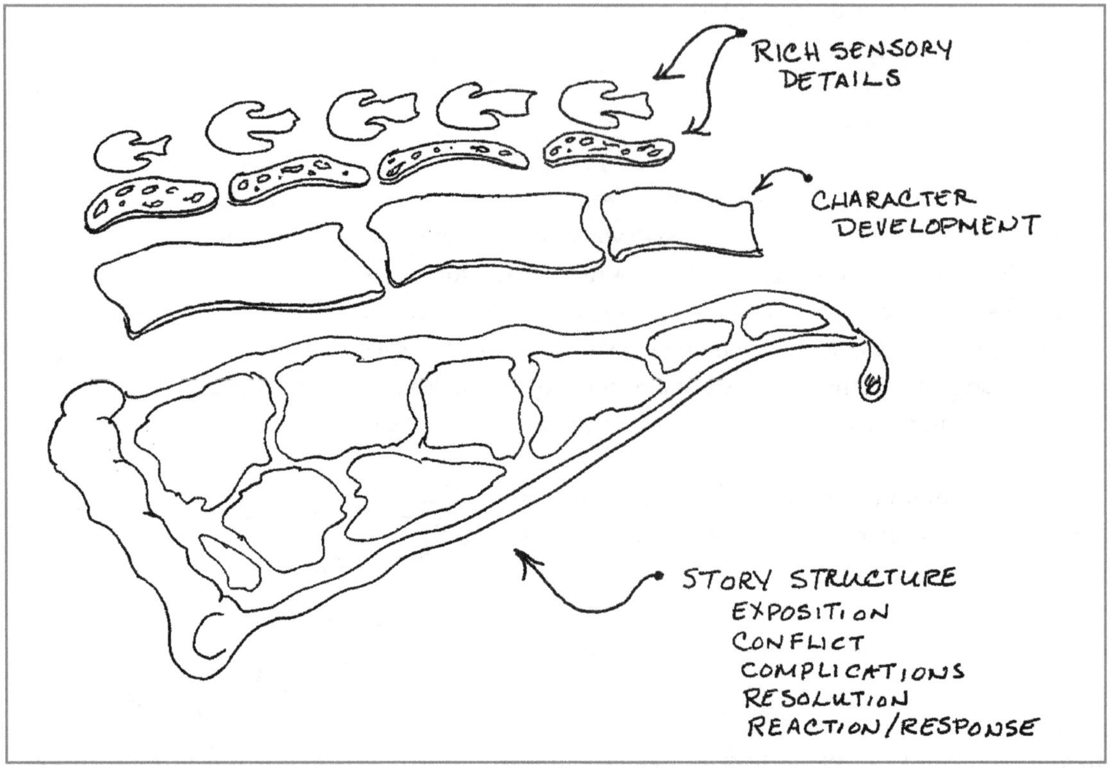

FIGURE 5.1. The "narrative pizza" organizational structure.

lessons would work against everything she tried to promote when creating a genuine literacy environment in her classroom. If she were to follow the lessons as defined in the test preparation booklets, she would be teaching in a way that ran counter to the practices her university professor had sponsored in her methods courses.

The rigid and prescriptive nature of these lessons would work against everything she tried to promote when creating a genuine literacy environment in her classroom.

When Esmeralda expressed her frustration in her discussions with other teachers, they offered a wide mixture of responses and advice. Bob Tewkes, a veteran of twenty-three years of teaching, observed, "What are you worried about? At least the students will get *some* instruction in writing. That's more than they got a few years ago. What harm is there? Someone has already planned your lessons for you. It's a good situation: the kids learn, and you have to work less."

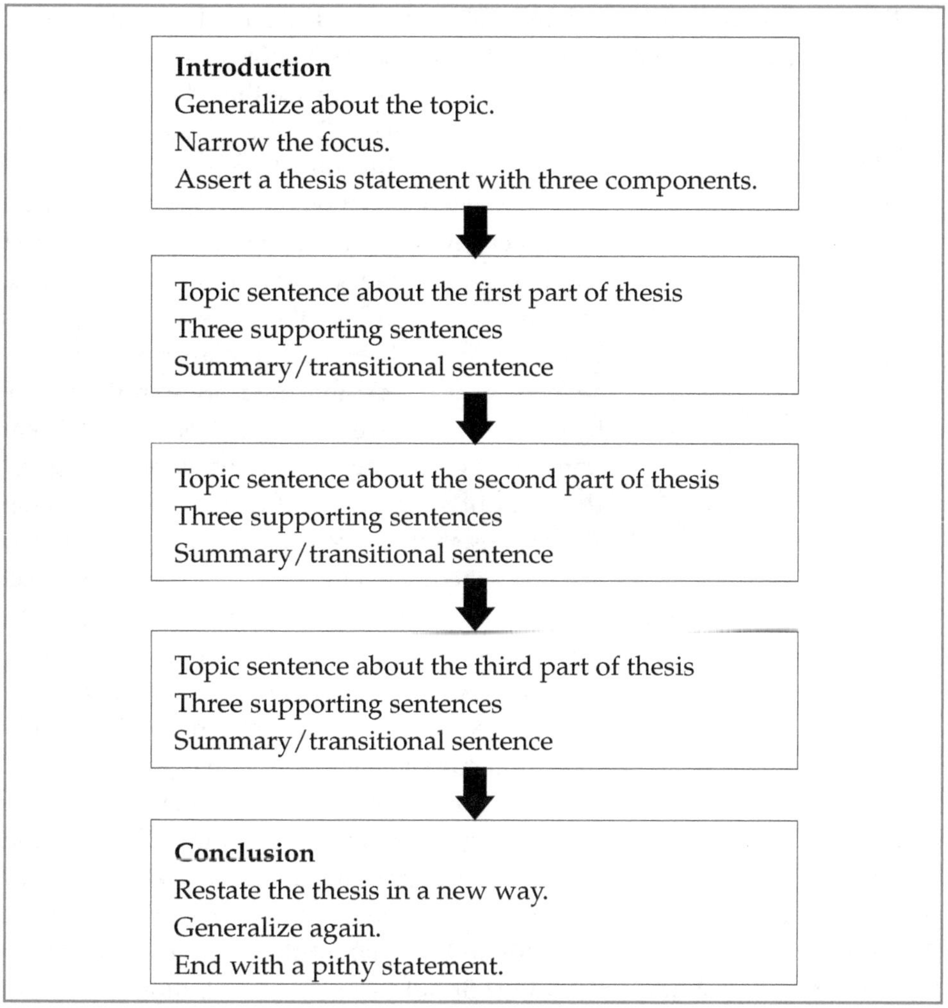

FIGURE 5.2. The "triangulation approach" to persuasive writing.

Maria Wilson, another veteran teacher, insisted, "I'm not putting up with this nonsense. I have no intention of using the test preparation booklets and drilling students to become mindless automatons. Writing demands *thinking*, and I'm going to teach students to *think*. I'll pick up the booklets from the principal's office, but I'll dump them in the garbage. I'd like to see someone force me to teach students to write by following a formula!"

Zlada Dzimtra, another first-year teacher, reported, "I'm not a tenured teacher. I'm in no position to defy anyone. I want to keep my job, so I'll do as I'm told. I know that the test preparation material promotes practices that are opposed to the way I was trained to teach writing, but I'll have to swallow my pride and do what is required."

Esmeralda understood the principal's concerns. The school had been on the state's academic watch list for the last two years. Ms. Bobbins was under a great deal of pressure to improve the school's scores on the state assessment. There is the real possibility that Eleanor Bobbins could be replaced as principal if the school remained on the academic watch list.

Ms. Bobbins was under a great deal of pressure to improve the school's scores on the state assessment. There is the real possibility that Eleanor Bobbins could be replaced as principal if the school remained on the academic watch list.

It seemed to Esmeralda that when teachers and students returned to school after the winter break, everything focused on the state exams. Posters mounted in the halls and in classrooms encouraged students to demonstrate pride in the school by performing well on the tests. The principal sent home a letter to parents and guardians to suggest the appropriate regimen of diet and sleep to help children reach their optimum test-taking state. Ms. Bobbins scheduled a motivational speaker to meet with the students in an all-school assembly during the week before the tests. Esmeralda learned from veteran teachers that last year's motivational speaker not only described the importance of academic achievement but also led cheers to promote enthusiasm for taking the required tests. In addition, the PTA would provide free high-protein breakfasts at school on the days of the tests.

For the next six weeks, Esmeralda would be expected to follow the lessons in the test preparation materials. During that time, she was sure to be observed by a supervisor. She resisted following the prescribed lessons, yet she felt the pressure to do what was required by the state and by the principal. **If you were Esmeralda, what would you do? Should she accept Bob's advice and follow the safe route that Zlada was taking? Should she be defiant, like Maria, and remain true to the research-supported methods she had learned in her teacher education program?**

Questions for Discussion

1. Does Esmeralda have an obligation to teach the way the principal prescribes and allow her instruction to be guided by a state-mandated test?
2. To what extent does Esmeralda have the academic freedom to design instruction that she judges to have the greatest educational value?
3. To what extent does each of Esmeralda's colleagues have a valid perspective and offer sound advice?

4. Could Esmeralda ignore the test preparation materials until a supervisor visits her classroom? If she could circumvent the principal's directives, would this be advisable? Explain.
5. Should Esmeralda and her colleagues meet with the principal to discuss their concerns about the use of the test preparation booklets? What would be the likely result of such a meeting?

Related Research and Writing

Research one of the following topics and share your findings with your classmates or colleagues.

1. Investigate the pressures in a local school to have teachers conform to a prescribed curriculum or to focus instruction on preparation for mandated tests. Interview a principal or teacher in a grade that must participate in state-mandated tests. How does the principal or teacher feel about the expectation to conform to the directives and standards that have been developed by people who might not be familiar with the school, its students, or its curriculum? To what extent does the individual teacher feel they have the freedom to provide the instruction they deem best? To what extent does the principal or teacher feel they are able to pursue the kind of instruction that seems to be the best in theory?
2. Interview teachers in a local school. To what extent do the teachers believe they have academic freedom? Does the school have an academic freedom committee? Does the school offer a written policy about academic freedom? What does the school do to safeguard academic freedom?
3. Read commentaries about mandated tests in your area. What arguments do supporters and detractors make about the mandated tests? Do the tests guide curriculum in a positive way? Do the tests provide important data about students? Do the tests allow schools to measure students' academic progress? Are the tests an important measure to hold schools and teachers accountable for quality instruction? Write your own position statement about the mandated tests, and share your position with classmates or colleagues.

6 It Can't Be This Difficult: Meaningful Peer Revision Activities

Preview: Any experienced English teacher will tell you that it can be a challenge to get students to think critically, particularly when it comes to their own writing or the writing of their peers. Students sometimes look for an easy way out, and if the opportunity is there, they may take it. The teacher in the following case discovers just how difficult it can be to get her students to be critical of their own and their peers' writing. Despite her best efforts, her students continue to resist putting real effort into learning and practicing the revising and editing skills she wants them to develop. What can this teacher do to help her students learn the value of and strategies for effective peer revision?

Focus Questions: As you read the following case, prepare to discuss the following questions: (1) Why is this teacher having so much trouble getting her students to think critically about their own writing and the writing of others? To what extent does the teacher contribute to her own problems? (2) What should the teacher do next to help her students become more thoughtful and critical of their own writing and the writing of others? What long-term plan might she use to develop and reinforce the critical thinking and revision strategies she wants her students to learn and use whenever they write and revise their own writing or read and respond to the writing of others?

The Case: It Can't Be This Difficult: Meaningful Peer Revision Activities

Lilly Compassa was frustrated. Even though she was only a first-year teacher, she judged that she was pretty strong when it came to the teaching of writing. She had attended a nearby state university that was known for its strong teaching-of-writing program. When Lilly was hired by Susan Lassiter, the principal of Abraham Lincoln Middle School, Susan had said, "Look, Lilly. I know you are inexperienced, but I'm hiring you because you seem to have some good ideas about how to teach writing. I'm assigning you to the eighth grade because that seems to be where we need the most work. Come and see me in a couple of months into the school year to let me know what you are doing and the progress you have made."

School had now been in session for almost two months, and Lilly hadn't seen much progress at all. She hadn't anticipated how difficult it would be to get her students to be thoughtful about revising, especially when it came to being critical of their own or other students' writing. In her teacher education program, she had taken a course that focused on teaching writing, and they had spent time talking about a writing process orientation and writing workshop, with collaborative revising and editing activities and why they are important. She had learned some strategies relevant to peer response and editing, and the professor had even made these activities a part of what students in the class were expected to do with their own writing. However, Lilly was learning that engaging in these activities with a group of preservice teachers was very different from trying to do them with a group of middle school students.

[Lilly] hadn't anticipated how difficult it would be to get her students to be thoughtful about revising, especially when it came to being critical of their own or other students' writing.

What frustrated Lilly most was that her students couldn't seem to comment constructively on their own or other students' writing. She had started by having them meet in small groups to read and discuss papers they had written about a field trip to the zoo. She asked the students to read their papers aloud one at a time, and then had the groups make comments on the strengths and areas for development of the writing. Unfortunately, after a few minutes most students were not on task, and it was clear that the group discussions focused more on social activities than on the strengths and areas for growth in the students' writing. Lilly tried to salvage the activity by refocusing it. After quieting the groups, she said, "You seem to be having some trouble, so I want you to read each piece of writing aloud and then pick the best one in the group. I'll come around to check on you and how you are doing. Does everyone understand what I want you to do?"

The refocused activity didn't go much better. One group would stay on task only if Lilly stood right there with them. A second group quickly read through the papers and picked the longest one because it had "a lot of details." A third group couldn't decide on the best and reported that they were all "really good." Another group picked the following composition as the best because, as Jaime, the spokesperson for his group, said, "It was short and to the point."

The Bayfed Zoo

I really liked the Bayfield zoo because it has alot of animals. My favorit is the lions because they are funy. I also liked the snakes. The piethon was awesome. Next to it a ratlesnake who was sheding his skin. Another animal I like is the elefants, I saw them fed them some hay and carots and other vegatables. I think we shuld go too the bayfeld zoo every day for school.

When Lilly asked the group about the grammar, spelling, and punctuation errors, Jaime said, "We knew what the writer meant. So what's the big deal?"

"I'll tell you what the big deal is!" Lilly started to say a little too loudly, but then she took a deep breath and instead said, "Class, you don't see how important it is that you learn how to be critical of writing. You don't seem to see how important the revision stage of the writing process is, so we are going to have to do some more work on this."

Lilly knew that her students needed more guidance, but she wasn't sure exactly what to do. That night she met with Delores Smith, a friend from her teacher education program who was teaching in a school district not far from Lilly's middle school. Delores seemed excited about the way her high school emphasized writing. When Lilly explained her problem, Delores said she understood that Lily's experience was typical for relatively inexperienced writers. Delores then said that most of the teachers in her school used various response activities to engage with students' writing. Revision was an ongoing process that involved regular conferences between writers and peer readers and the teacher. In Delores's class, students collaborated in creating different response guides based on their needs as writers and the specific contexts for writing; the act of writing in conversation with others was a normal part of her classroom culture.

Revision was an ongoing process that involved regular conferences between writers and peer readers and the teacher.

This approach was different from her own, but Lilly saw some promise in it. In fact, Lilly wondered whether she should make students take some responsibility for others' writing, something similar to the writing work in Delores's class; maybe students' grades on some writing assignments would be contingent on how well they evaluated other students' writing. Lilly got excited, imagining how this might motivate her students to take revision and editing more seriously.

Delores wrapped up the conversation by saying, "Before I started the school year and knew more about the framework for writing at my school, I paid for something online at that popular teacher site, BuyMyCurriculum. It's an evaluation sheet that might work for you, if you think the goal is for students to learn the criteria for producing effective writing and be able to apply those criteria when they evaluate their own or peer writing." Delores forwarded the evaluation sheet to Lilly when she got home (see Figure 6.1). Lilly had high hopes that this particular tool might help her with her problem.

Descriptive Writing Evaluation Sheet

Evaluator's Name: ___________________________
Author's Name: _____________________________

Directions: Put a check next to the sentence that best describes how well the writer performs in each of the following five areas: Focus, elaboration, dialogue, language, and mechanics.

I. Focus

_____ Clear and sharp with strong impact—details all work to create an overall impression
_____ Sometimes marred by material that is irrelevant or that does not contribute to the central impression
_____ Tends to jump from one idea to another—does not create an overall impression

II. Elaboration

_____ Good use of specific, concrete detail
_____ Includes a variety of sensory imagery
_____ Uses some effective figurative language (simile, metaphor, personification, etc.)
_____ Uses some specific, concrete detail but needs to include more
_____ Includes some descriptions that are clichéd (overused and unoriginal)
_____ Includes very little specific, concrete detail
_____ Includes many clichés
_____ Needs to include more variety of sensory imagery (sound, touch, taste, smell, sight)
_____ Needs to include more figurative language (simile, metaphor, personification, etc.)

III. Dialogue (If applicable)

_____ Effective use of direct dialogue
_____ Some effective use of direct dialogue
_____ Needs to use direct dialogue more often when people are conversing
_____ Needs to use direct dialogue when people are conversing

IV. Language

_____ Effective word choice ("The child lazily waddled down the street.")
_____ Satisfactory word choice ("The child lazily walked down the street.")
_____ Weak word choice ("The child went down the street.")

V. Mechanics, Usage, Spelling, etc.

_____ Good
_____ Satisfactory
_____ Weak

Grade I would give the composition: _____

FIGURE 6.1. Delores's descriptive writing evaluation sheet for peer review.

The following morning, over coffee, Lilly discussed her problem with Aaron Worth, one of the other eighth-grade language arts teachers. After explaining what had happened in class, Lilly summed it up this way: "They just wouldn't get serious about being critical of their own or one another's writing. I guess I sort of assumed that they had done peer evaluation before and I wouldn't need to tell them everything. Have you got any ideas about what I might try next?"

"I think you're right, Lilly," Aaron said. "They probably do need more guidance. I like to type out one or two paragraphs and walk them through what I want them to do when they respond to a friend's writing. I really believe in modeling strategies. I just happen to have a mocked-up paragraph and some notes that I planned to use later today. You are welcome to try it yourself. I'll email you a copy right now," he said, opening his laptop.

"Thanks, Aaron. I really appreciate it."

Lilly opened her email on her phone when Aaron left the English office and pulled up his paragraph. It looked good, and Lilly made up her mind about what she was going to do. She dropped the text into the class shared drive, keeping the notes separate. She then spent the next few minutes planning out her activity using Aaron's paragraph and the evaluation sheet Dolores had sent her. When class started, she asked students to pull up the paragraph (see Figure 6.2) and evaluation sheet (Figure 6.1), indicated that the sample had been written by an unnamed eighth-grade student in another class, and asked her students to read it and evaluate it using the evaluation sheet.

After the activity, when she asked several students to read their comments, they ranged from overly critical to neutral to "It's very good. I like it." None of the comments was specific enough to the text to be useful to the writer, and far too many dealt with minor mechanical errors. One of her weakest spellers even managed to find four misspellings that were not in the paragraph. Another student focused only on fixing usage that the reader judged to be "just bad English." Then there was a student whose most helpful comment was, "It's booooring." Lilly concluded that her students were not yet ready to be turned loose onto rethinking their own or evaluating others' papers.

None of the comments was specific enough to the text to be useful to the writer, and far too many dealt with minor mechanical errors.

As Lilly left the classroom that day, she wondered what had gone wrong. Had she provided too much guidance or structure? Had she overwhelmed the students with too many things to consider? Perhaps they hadn't worked enough with descriptive writing to understand what was meant by "specific details," "figurative language," or some of the other terminology. Maybe she just hadn't

Second Floor LRC

I gotta think of a topic to write, I can hear the sounds of whispering people behind me. I look up and I can see many colors of cloths with people, whom I havent met, in them. Now someone clumpes along the floor, then that same person whirls the pencil sharpenor over the pencil. Satisfied, they walk away. I hear the teacher mumbling something about divisin as they help someone with a math problem. I hear a jingle and I turn around to see the janiter behind me picking papers as they go along. Someone giggles and I stop thinking for a minute. The buzing sound of the lights above is bugging me. Now I hear the sound, somewhat like a zipper, of someone tearing a sheet of pape from there spiral notebook. The hum of the bell reminds me I'm about to leave. Study period is over. I'm finna rush down the staris to lunch.

FIGURE 6.2. Aaron's sample student writing paragraph.

pushed them enough to explain and defend their responses. Maybe these students weren't mature enough to handle being critical of writing. She wondered whether her students would *ever* learn to be critical of their own and others' writing. She also wondered what she would report to the principal, who wanted to hear about the progress of Lilly's students. **What else could she do? If you were in Lilly's situation, what would you do?**

Questions for Discussion

1. How would you explain why the teacher is having so much trouble getting her students to learn how to be critical of their own and their peers' writing?
2. To what extent does Lilly contribute to the problems her students are having? In other words, what mistakes, if any, does she make? How could she correct some mistakes?
3. Lilly starts a frustrated response to Jaime when he makes what seems to be a snarky remark about grammar, spelling, and punctuation, but then she backs off and makes a general comment to the class. Was this the right strategy? Why or why not?
4. What would you have done differently the day Lilly used another teacher's paragraph and evaluation sheet? Why? If you were Aaron or Delores, and Lilly approached you about what happened in class that day, what would you say to her? Why?
5. If Susan Lassiter, the principal, asks Lilly how she is doing with the writing program, what should she say? Why? Is it likely that the principal will be

critical of Lilly's performance? Do you think the principal has a responsibility to help Lilly with her situation? Why or why not? Do you think the principal was asking too much of Lilly in this situation? Why or why not?

6. One major difference between Lilly's and Delores's situations is that at Delores's school there is a department-wide agreement that writing is an ongoing and social experience that includes a significant emphasis on agency, authenticity, and honoring students' various writing processes. How important is it that an English department or school-wide writing program place a high priority on these elements rather than on, say, grammatical correctness in student writing?
7. What short-term and long-term solutions can you devise for Lilly? What is the best course of action for her to take? Why?

Related Research and Writing

Select one of the following areas of investigation, research the topic, and produce a brief written report that you can share with other students in your class or with your colleagues.

1. Read a book published by the National Council of Teachers of English, the National Writing Project, or another education-focused press that discusses strategies for engaging students in writing processes and learning how to write. What are the strengths and weaknesses of the book's approach? Do you think the methods or strategies would be effective with students? Why or why not?
2. Talk to an experienced middle school or high school English teacher about problems they have had with inviting students to be critical of their own and others' writing. What are the major problem areas? Why? How have they addressed these problems?
3. Examine a few articles that suggest different approaches or strategies for coaching students through revising and editing writing. Who are some of the most influential proponents of peer review? What are some of the most promising approaches or strategies? Why? How do these methods get students to be thoughtful about or critical of their own and others' writing?

7

Out of Control: Delinquent or Disabled?

Preview: Occasionally, a teacher will experience a class or a particular student who poses significant challenges for the orderly management of students and instruction. The teacher ponders why students are disruptive and uncooperative and struggles to figure out how to correct unruly behavior while still maintaining a positive rapport with students and a supportive classroom environment. In the following case, a teacher feels some dread about meeting with her class and worries about the options available to her to correct a bad situation. She will have to draw on what she knows about the psychology of adolescents and invoke whatever help and resources are available within the school.

Focus Questions: As you study the following case, keep these questions in mind: (1) Does the teacher face a significant problem? How do you know whether the problem is serious or superficial? (2) Why has the problem occurred? (3) What can the teacher do to keep her class productive and cooperative so that she no longer dreads each class meeting?

The Case: Out of Control: Delinquent or Disabled?

Although it was a cool October morning and the faculty workroom was a chilly fifty-eight degrees, Karen Moskovitz could feel perspiration build on her forehead and upper lip. She was almost physically ill contemplating the prospect of facing her unruly third-period sophomore English class. It seemed that several forces combined to make the third period the worst possible learning environment.

The class met in the late morning, when adolescents were beginning to wake up and become lively. The students had not yet gone to lunch, so they were usually hungry. The class included several students with various learning challenges. In fact, almost everyone in class had some sort of significant learning challenge. Five students had active individualized education programs (IEPs).

Four others had been identified as having attention deficit disorder (ADD) or attention deficit/hyperactivity disorder (ADHD). These students had their own accommodation plans. Two other students were in the school's Title 1 reading program, which meant that they had significant difficulty with reading and a pronounced reluctance to read. Three other students were making a transition from English as a second language (ESL) classes to a mainstream English class. Since English was their second language, they lacked confidence and struggled to follow directions and complete assignments. One student was a recent immigrant from Lithuania. Although he knew little English, his parents insisted that he participate in a mainstream English class rather than an ESL class.

Frequently, Karen found herself shouting above the general din of the class in an attempt to achieve some order.

With all of these learning challenges and the plans and accommodations that other school personnel had written for the students, Karen was overwhelmed by the multiple details and interventions she was supposed to attend to. And almost every day the students were excitable and restless. They couldn't sit still in their seats, they said aloud whatever was on their minds whenever they wanted, and they seldom paid attention to directions. Karen could not rely on students to complete homework or to bring the appropriate materials to class. Frequently, Karen found herself shouting above the general din of the class in an attempt to achieve some order. After third period on most days, Karen felt completely worn out and defeated.

The most disturbing element of the class was the behavior of a student named Darrell. Although Darrell didn't have an accommodation plan, his counselor reported that the family physician had diagnosed him as ADHD and had prescribed regular doses of a medication that was supposed to help him focus. Karen, however, found Darrell completely incorrigible. During every class meeting, she repeatedly corrected him for turning around in his desk to disturb the student behind him. Karen would have moved him to a seat where he would be away from distractions, but every location in the classroom seemed to pose a distraction. He compulsively talked out of turn, with comments that had little or no relevance to the focus of the lesson. If he felt like talking to someone across the room, he simply shouted above any other discussion. If he felt like looking out the window, tossing something in the wastebasket, or sharpening a pencil, he immediately followed his impulse. Karen corrected Darrell repeatedly, but he appeared oblivious to attempts to control his behavior. Karen decided that part of his problem was the fact that his regular dose of medication did not occur until after her class.

Lately, Darrell has become more belligerent to Karen's attempts to correct his behavior. If she makes simple requests, like directing him to take out this book, he argues with her. His responses have taken this form: "Why do I need to take out the book? I'm not going to read it anyway. It's a stupid book." If Karen directs Darrell to stop talking or turning around, he responds, "Why are you always picking on me? You don't say anything to anyone else."

"His hyperactivity is his disability. I can't very well punish him for a behavioral disability any more than I can punish a student for having a physical disability."

Karen has talked to Darrell's mother several times. She seems sympathetic but reports that Darrell's behavior is connected to a physical disorder that she is trying to control with medication. His mother too seems to be at a loss to change Darrell's behavior. Karen has given Darrell detentions, but he usually doesn't show up. She has sent him to the dean on a discipline referral, but the dean has done little more than scold Darrell and send him back to class. After Darrell missed three opportunities to serve a detention, the dean gave him a one-day in-school suspension. The dean told Karen, "There's not much I can do. His hyperactivity is his disability. I can't very well punish him for a behavioral disability any more than I can punish a student for having a physical disability."

There are two aspects of Darrell's behavior that Karen finds particularly disturbing at this point. She knows that his behavior is a distraction to the rest of the class. When Darnell is absent, the class has a much more purposeful, orderly, and cooperative atmosphere. It is clear that he has a negative impact on the learning of all the students. Second, Karen fears that Darrell's responses to her and to his classmates will become more volatile. She has yet to witness any violent behavior from Darrell, but she senses from his combative behavior with her that he is capable of becoming violent if provoked. And it is hard to predict what Darrell might find provocative.

Karen has followed the usual course of interventions. She corrected Darrell in class; she spoke to him outside of class about his behavior; she assigned detentions; she spoke to the parent; she referred the student to the dean. Karen feels that she has run out of options. Although she believes that she has taken all the reasonable courses of action in an effort to manage her class, she worries that if her supervisor were to observe the class, she would judge Karen as a weak teacher who has allowed the class to run out of control. At the end of her next planning period, Karen will face Darrell and the rest of her challenging third-period class. There is bound to be trouble. **How should she respond when Darrell acts up again today? What long-term intervention can she put in place to help Darrell and the rest of the class for the balance of the school year?**

Questions for Discussion

1. Why do you judge that Darrell acts the way he does? Do you suppose it is possible for him to control his behavior, or for his behavior to be controlled?
2. Explain whether or not Karen has exhausted all the means available to her to manage her class. What more, if anything, could Karen have done? Would any other action on her part have had a different effect?
3. What can Karen do immediately to bring her unruly class under control and avoid an ugly confrontation?
4. If you were Karen, could you solicit the aid of any other school personnel—the nurse? a counselor? her supervisor? another teacher? What help could any of these other individuals provide? What, if anything, could be the negative consequences of inviting help from others?
5. To what extent would it be useful for Karen to seek to have Darrell removed from her class? Is his removal a realistic possibility? What would be the disadvantages, if any, to removing Darrell?
6. Devise a long-term plan for Karen to help her create a more orderly and productive atmosphere in her class and to help her cope with a very stressful situation. Who would be involved with this plan? What actions should she take? What makes you think any new measures would help?

Related Research and Writing

Research one of the following topics and share your findings with your classmates or colleagues.

1. Write your own case study to describe a challenging student or disruptive class that you have witnessed during the thousands of hours you have spent in schools. What was done to try to correct the situation? What efforts were helpful? What efforts seemed to have little positive effect? What could anyone have done better to handle the situation?
2. Interview an experienced teacher about a class or a student who has posed considerable management problems. In writing, recount the situation for your colleagues. What interventions did the teacher try? What worked? What did not work? How does the teacher account for the relative efficaciousness of the actions?

3. Read about children who are labeled *behavioral disordered*. How is this condition defined? To what extent does the label seem an appropriate and accurate name for a student's condition? What are the signs or symptoms that would allow someone to identify a student as behaviorally disordered? If the student has been identified as having such a disability, to what extent must a teacher treat the classroom behavioral issues differently than they would with a less challenging class?

8 It's Just a Soccer Game: How Will These Students View Me?

Preview: Sometimes it's hard to navigate the teacher-student relationship. Some young teachers are fairly close in age to high school seniors, which in a way invites a casual familiarity. In their roles as coaches and club advisors, teachers meet students under more relaxed conditions, and there is a natural inclination to develop a friendly rapport. Even teachers who are quite distant in age from their learners cannot help but develop a fondness and closeness with students. In the following case, a young teacher must decide when a close relationship with students might become an impediment to his role as teacher. He must determine whether it would be best for him to distance himself from students, even at the risk of being thought uptight or aloof.

Focus Questions: As you study the following case, consider the following questions: (1) Is Willie Stover in a dangerous situation? What, if anything, does he have to worry about? (2) Should Willie investigate anything before he acts? What, if anything, would he investigate? How would he proceed? (3) What should Willie's immediate course of action be? Does he need to devise a policy for the future? If he does, what would it be?

The Case: It's Just a Soccer Game: How Will These Students View Me?

Willie Stover had been looking forward to this Saturday afternoon. He was an enthusiastic soccer fan. He enjoyed soccer in many ways—as a player, as a coach, and as a spectator. At Gompers East, a suburban high school where Willie taught English, his soccer enthusiasm and experience had landed him the job as girls varsity soccer coach. On this particular weekend, Willie had invited two of his close friends to his apartment in the city to watch Tottenham Hotspur and Manchester United, two of the top teams in the English Premier League. Willie's friends, Marcus Striker and Dylan Medfield, both in their early twenties, remained at the apartment while Willie ran to the store for more beer and snacks. All the pieces were falling into place for a great afternoon of soccer viewing.

When Willie returned with bags of beer, tortilla chips, and pork rinds, there was no place to park in front of the building, and he was forced to double-park as he unloaded. After Willie climbed the stairs and opened the door to his apartment, he was met with a surprise. Leslie and Makalya, two senior members of the Gompers East girls varsity soccer team, were sitting in Willie's living room with his two friends. As Willie stepped into the room, it appeared to him that he was interrupting an animated conversation between his friends and the students. One look at Marcus and Dylan told Willie that his friends were delighted with the company of Leslie and Makalya, who could easily be mistaken for mature college students. "Surprised to see us, Mr. Stover?" asked Leslie.

As Willie stepped into the room, it appeared to him that he was interrupting an animated conversation between his friends and the students.

"You *could* say that," replied Willie, as he nearly dropped a bag of beer on the floor.

"We've been enjoying the company of these two visitors," said Marcus.

"What are you doing here?" Willie asked the girls.

"We came to watch the game with the world's biggest soccer fan," said Makalya.

Anticipating Willie's response, Leslie said, "Don't make us go, Mr. Stover. I texted my dad and he said we could stay. We're just going to watch the game and then we're on our way."

"Come on, Mr. Stover," said Makayla. "Don't be weird about it!"

"You're not making us leave now, Mr. S., not after we drove all the way into the city," Leslie insisted.

"We'll see," said Willie. He put the beer and snacks in the kitchen and made his way downstairs to move his car, giving him a little time to ponder this awkward situation—and there *was* a lot to think about.

Leslie's words echoed in Willie's head: "Don't be weird about it!" In his first two years of teaching at Gompers East, he had developed a strong bond with the students. In general, he felt that the students liked him—the students in his classes, the students on his soccer team, even students he didn't know. There were several reasons for the rapport: He was one of the younger teachers in the school, he could talk to students candidly about the things that interest them, and he avoided being severely judgmental. Willie remembered one student's assessment on his course evaluation: "You are awesome, Mr. S. You are not uptight like the other teachers."

As Willie got into his car, he wondered if there was any possible way he could allow the players to stay. If the girls had indeed gotten permission, there might be nothing to worry about. But Willie hadn't actually talked to any adults himself. He wondered, "Could I call them myself and get permission from each over the phone?" One complication was that Leslie's parents were divorced. Could he accept permission from just one parent?

If the girls had indeed gotten permission, there might be nothing to worry about. But Willie hadn't actually talked to any adults himself.

If Willie insisted that the players leave, he knew that from that moment forward he would be "a dud," as some on the team labeled one of the school's rule-obsessed teachers. In the minds of his team and those of most of his students, he would have joined the ranks of the decidedly uncool veteran teachers, separating himself from the lives of his students by refusing to take a chance. If he didn't allow the players to stay, how would he actually get rid of them? Leslie would be difficult. She was always challenging authority and was liable to hold on to a sofa leg and dare him to drag her away!

As he slowly circled the block, Willie called his Aunt Honora, who had taught elementary school for thirty years. When he described the situation to her, Aunt Honora did not hesitate: "Get those girls out of there right now, Willie. You are just looking for trouble. Those kids may be perfectly naive and innocent, but I don't know that your friends are. You've got to think about the impression their presence is going to make on people who learn about the students' visit." Willie knew his aunt was right, but he had to figure out what, precisely, he was going to do.

Willie pulled his car into an open parking space at the end of the block. As he paced down the street, he remembered his friends' eagerness to have Leslie and Makalya stay to watch the soccer match. To them, the players were just two attractive young women, not high school students. It seemed perfectly natural to have them stay to enjoy the match.

Willie ascended the stairs to his apartment and wondered, "When I open that door, what am I going to do?" **If you were in Willie's position, what would *you* do?**

Questions for Discussion

1. Willie is concerned about the presence of the students. What is at risk? What is the basis for his concern?

2. If Willie wanted to resolve some of the doubts he has, how would he proceed?
3. Should Willie be concerned about the opinions and feelings of his students if he insists that his unexpected visitors leave? How will his decision affect the rapport he has with his students in the future?
4. If the two students resist leaving the apartment, how can Willie convince them to depart?
5. If the two students genuinely have permission to stay, should Willie let them? Explain how you have arrived at your decision.
6. When Willie returns to his apartment, what should he do? Explain why you think this course of action is best.
7. What assumptions are we making about age, gender identity, sexuality, and even marital status as we consider Willie's actions? How do those assumptions shape our recommendations?

Related Research and Writing

Research one of the following topics and share your findings with your classmates or colleagues.

1. Discuss with someone at a local school the policy that should guide a teacher's behavior regarding contact with students outside of class. For example, are teachers cautioned not to give students rides home after athletic practice or other extracurricular events? Are teachers advised not to meet with students outside of class time? If teachers do have conferences with students outside of class, what precautions must teachers take?
2. Interview a young teacher about any difficulty they have had in balancing a teacher persona and a friend persona when dealing with friendly and likeable students. What challenges has the teacher experienced? To what extent were the difficulties the product of the teacher's relative youth? How has the teacher managed to maintain a balance without compromising their integrity?
3. Recall any close relationships you have had with teachers or coaches. Were there ever times when you sensed the teacher trying to maintain some personal distance? Were there ever times when the teacher or you were uncomfortable with the apparently friendly rapport? Do you recall any teacher who appeared to be too friendly with students? What was the effect of being too friendly?

9

First Observation

Preview: Most teachers find the process of observation and evaluation of their classroom performance to be stressful. The visitation by a school administrator is bound to change the climate in the classroom, and it is difficult to proceed as though no visitor were there. It is also stressful to think that someone will make a judgment about your performance and your worth as a teacher.

Focus Questions: As you study the following case, consider these questions: (1) How should a teacher prepare for a classroom observation by a school administrator? (2) Should a teacher adjust any plans and usual practices when expecting a classroom visit?

The Case: First Observation

Lance Southey's department chair had already made one uneventful informal observation of his teaching, but when the chair scheduled a formal observation in early October, Lance broke into a cold sweat. He didn't perceive Helen Bastion, the English department chair, as an aggressive, intimidating person, so at first it was difficult for him to understand his sense of panic about being observed and evaluated. Perhaps it was because he respected and admired Ms. Bastion that he cared a great deal about winning her respect, which placed inordinate significance on the observation.

As Lance reflected on his reaction to the scheduled observation, he recognized several sources for his apprehension. First, three new teachers had been hired for the current school year. When the three teachers were hired, the personnel director noted that one position was a replacement for someone on maternity leave. The veteran teacher was sure to return after her one-year leave of absence, and only two of the three new teachers would be retained. Lance felt that each observation would be a kind of audition for a job in competition with the other two first-year teachers. It didn't help also that Lela Cahill, an accounting teacher and notorious rumormonger in the high school, had commented about Lance's first observation: "You better watch out, kiddo. Bastion is pretty tough. If she's determined to weed you out of her department, you're a goner. She's already driven a couple of people into early retirement."

Lance felt that each observation would be a kind of audition for a job in competition with the other two first-year teachers.

Second, Lance had initially felt adequately prepared to teach high school English; but when he talked to veteran teachers on the staff at Park Forest High School, he began to doubt that he knew much about teaching at all. Everyone else seemed knowledgeable, prepared, and confident. Lance worried that when Ms. Bastion came to observe, she would recognize his many pedagogical inadequacies.

Ms. Bastion had asked to visit Lance's ninth-grade class of struggling readers, which met in the early afternoon, right after lunch. She scheduled the visit for a Friday during the school's Homecoming week, apparently the only time she could visit in early October. Lance would have preferred that the department chair visit a different class, but he felt he wasn't in a position to refuse. The class could be cooperative and fun, but on some days, especially if a distracting incident had occurred at lunch, the students arrived to class in a hyperactive state and couldn't settle down to focus on the lesson. Lance worried that the class could go either way—cooperative or wild. In fact, he assumed that Ms. Bastion's presence would be enough of a distraction to potentially trigger the students' hyperactivity. As Lance projected what he would be doing in class on the day of the visit, he recognized that he had planned a rather complicated structure as a way to prompt students to discuss related themes in a series of poems.

Everyone else seemed knowledgeable, prepared, and confident. Lance worried that when Ms. Bastion came to observe, she would recognize his many pedagogical inadequacies.

Lance turned to two mentors for help. Arthur Jelinek was the official mentor the school district had assigned to Lance as part of the formal mentoring program. Arthur, who had taught in the district for thirty years, was a nice person who had been helpful to Lance in many ways at the beginning of the school year, patiently reviewing practices in taking attendance and introducing Lance to the important people he should know in the building. In addition, Elaine Kucnarczyk had become an *informal* mentor. Lance gravitated to her because of her keen intelligence and pleasant demeanor. He felt comfortable talking to Elaine about his lesson designs and his concerns about particular students. When Lance shared his apprehension with his two mentors, each one offered advice about how he might approach his first formal observation and evaluation.

When Lance shared his apprehension with his two mentors, each one offered advice about how he might approach his first formal observation and evaluation.

Arthur counseled Lance in this way: "I'm going to tell you what to do. I can share with you a vocabulary activity that kids just love. Actually, it's a vocabulary *game*. It's all explained in a handout. Kids have to work together to complete the activity. The students will be *active*. It's just the kind of thing Helen loves. The beauty of the vocabulary activity is that you can use it at any time. All students need to develop their vocabulary all the time. It's a sure-fire lesson. I'll put a copy in your mailbox."

Elaine suggested another approach: "Don't diverge from your instructional plan for the lesson that Helen will observe. She will most likely want to meet with you before the observation to discuss your plan. She might be able to suggest some fine-tuning of the plan. Let Helen see what you can do, and let her make some recommendations. I don't think you want to do something that wouldn't ordinarily be part of your lesson. Take some chances. Don't play it safe. Let Helen see you for the teacher you are. I know you want to develop as a teacher, and it's Helen's job to support your development."

Lance was left with a few choices. He could play it safe and use Arthur's "surefire" lesson. He could take some chances by pursuing a lesson that was consistent with his overall plan but might pose some problems for student engagement and management. In addition, he could probably approach Ms. Bastion about rescheduling the observation. **If you were in Lance's position, what would you do?**

Questions for Discussion

1. Is it possible and advisable for Lance to try to reschedule the observation? What would be gained if he rescheduled?
2. What can Lance do to relieve the pressure of the situation enough that he can perform naturally and confidently?
3. Evaluate the advice offered by Lance's two mentors. Which mentor, if either, offers the most reasonable advice? Why?
4. What lesson options are available to Lance? Could he take an approach that neither Arthur nor Elaine considered? What approach would that be?

5. To what extent has Lance placed too much pressure on himself? Is this actually a relatively inconsequential situation? Explain.

Related Research and Writing

Select one of the following areas of investigation, research the topic, and produce a brief written report you can share with your colleagues.

1. Read the teacher evaluation plan for a school to which you have access. What are the steps involved in the evaluation of teachers? What criteria do evaluators use to judge the quality of a teacher's performance? Are the criteria clear and do they provide a valid standard for performance? What is the stated purpose of the evaluation system?
2. Search the professional literature to identify what other thinkers offer as indicators of quality teaching. Find at least three articles that describe exemplary teacher behaviors. Identify some similarities or recurring themes among the articles. Summarize your findings and share them with your classmates or colleagues.
3. Interview a relatively new teacher and a veteran teacher. Ask them to describe the teacher evaluation system in their schools. What has been their experience with teacher evaluation? Do they find the process a worthwhile one that encourages their professional growth? Do they view the process as an unnecessary intrusion? If they are rated, what is their reaction to the rating? Summarize what you have learned from your interviews and share your observations with your classmates or colleagues.

10

Doing the Right Thing

Preview: While they may not receive the same respect or status as other professionals in our society, teachers have a long history of being held to a higher professional ethical standard and personal conduct standard than professionals in other fields. This case examines the ethical responsibilities of a teacher who observes another teacher engaging in questionable behavior and also encouraging new teachers to engage in the same behavior. Under what circumstances must a teacher step in to put a stop to unethical behavior by another teacher?

Focus Questions: As you study the case, consider the following questions: (1) How should the teacher in this case respond when she encounters another teacher talking about one of her students in a derogatory manner and encouraging other teachers to do the same? (2) To what extent does a teacher have an ethical responsibility to stop unethical behavior on the part of another teacher when the observer is not directly involved in the unethical behavior?

The Case: Doing the Right Thing

When Rebecca Hart, a sixth-year English teacher, entered the teachers' lounge after her fifth-period class, all she wanted was a few minutes of peace and quiet during her preparation time before her last-period class. Everyone has bad days, and for Rebecca this had certainly been one of them. A fight had broken out in the hallway near her first-period classroom just before the bell rang, and she, along with another teacher, had had to break it up before anything serious happened. Fortunately, the two boys involved in the fight seemed to be more interested in acting tough than in actually landing a punch. However, she ended up having to take the boys down to the office, and, as a result, her first-period class got started late, and she had trouble getting the class settled down. Then, two periods later, a student set off a fire alarm, sending everyone outside into a cold drizzle for nearly twenty minutes. The next class period was a nightmare. She had trouble getting the kids in her ninth-grade "essentials" class to settle down; and when she finally did, the peace lasted only a few minutes. She spent most of the period using just about every strategy she knew to keep them quiet and on task. As a result, by the end of fifth period, Rebecca was exhausted and ready for a little quiet time.

When she entered the teachers' lounge, Rebecca was a little disappointed when she saw that Lucile Browning, a veteran English teacher, was in an animated conversation with Mary Okawa, a first-year English teacher. Lucile could sometimes get loud, especially when she started complaining about things—the government, the school administration, and sometimes even her students. Rebecca's thoughts were on the hope of a quiet moment, so she headed for a chair as far away from the pair as she could reasonably get. Fortunately, there were only two other teachers in the lounge, so she didn't have trouble finding a place to sit. Rebecca took a folder with some papers she needed to grade out of her bag and tried to focus on the top paper.

Lucile could sometimes get loud, especially when she started complaining about things—the government, the school administration, and sometimes even her students.

"That kid's a real problem! What a thug!" Rebecca overheard Lucile say to Mary.

"Really?" Mary inquired.

"And he's as dumb as a fence post. I really tore into his last essay. He can't write a simple English sentence. He's signed up for speech next semester, Mary, so being our resident new speech teacher, you'll probably get him in your class. Watch out! You'll have one heck of a time getting him to pass."

"He can't be all that bad," Mary said.

"Hey, Chuck! Don't you agree that this kid's a jerk?" Lucile suddenly shouted from across the room. "Isn't he in your biology class?"

Charles "Chuck" Castro, a first-year biology teacher, looked up from the student lab reports he was grading and somewhat hesitantly responded that the student in question was in his third-period biology class. Rebecca was more than a little irritated. She needed quiet, but more important, she did not like the direction this discussion was taking. Complaining about students to others was bad enough, but holding court with two impressionable new teachers was going too far. Also, encouraging Chuck to complain about the student was totally unprofessional. Rebecca wondered if it was too late to get up and leave before things got any worse.

"Come on, Chuck, admit it. The kid can't be trusted. Am I right? I bet he's pulled some things on you, hasn't he?"

Complaining about students to others was bad enough, but holding court with two impressionable new teachers was going too far.

"Well, now that you mention it, there was this one time when he and this other kid asked for a pass to go to the washroom, and they were gone for most of the period," Chuck said.

"And what happened when they came back and you called them on it?" Lucile asked. "I bet he made some smart remark like he usually does to me."

"Well, . . ." Chuck started to say.

Rebecca sighed and looked down at the paper she was attempting to grade; she knew she would have to make a decision. **If you were in Rebecca's situation, what would you do?**

Questions for Discussion

1. Rebecca is not directly involved in the conversation about the student, so how does she have any responsibility to say or do anything in this situation? Can't she just get up and leave? Why or why not?
2. Rebecca has had a particularly difficult day, and given her need to get herself together for her last-period class, should her most immediate concern be prepping for her class? Why or why not?
3. To what extent does Rebecca, or any teacher for that matter, have an ethical obligation to take action when she sees another experienced teacher acting in an unprofessional manner in front of inexperienced teachers and encouraging them to act in an unprofessional manner?
4. While stopping what is happening now by immediately confronting Lucile about her inappropriate behavior might seem like the best thing to do, perhaps Rebecca should take her concerns to her department chair or another administrator. To what extent would such a consultation be useful? What is likely to result? What would you recommend?
5. Lucile complains about all sorts of things, so why bother saying anything to her about her inappropriate actions? If Rebecca gets involved at all, should she just take the two new teachers aside and tell them why it is inappropriate to make comments about students as well as to encourage others to do the same? Why or why not?

6. What is the appropriate action for Rebecca in this situation? Why is that the right thing for her to do? What are the possible disadvantages associated with your recommended course of action? What are the potential benefits?

Related Research and Writing

Select one of the following areas of investigation, research the topic, and produce a brief written report you can share with your colleagues.

1. Use an index of education journals to search for articles that discuss professionalism and ethical standards for teachers. What standards do commentators offer to guide teachers in their ethical conduct in school and out of school?
2. Discuss with your classmates or colleagues their expectations for teachers' professional behavior. What kinds of behaviors do people find unacceptable in teachers? Guided by your discussions, devise your own code of ethical conduct that you can share with others.
3. Interview teachers, parents, and administrators who are connected with a local school or with the school you attended as a student. Find out if the school has expectations for teachers' ethical and professional behavior. For example, are there specific expectations for respecting confidentiality about grades, medical conditions, and other information available in student records? Are teachers allowed to use students' written work in class to show examples of deficient performance? How do leaders in the school convey the expectations to staff? What part do parents play in defining standards of conduct for teachers? Tell your classmates or colleagues what you have learned as an example of how a school might set standards for ethical conduct and train the staff in those standards.

11

Copycat

Preview: Teachers often express concern about students plagiarizing. In some instances, the fault is the students' ignorance of the obligation to cite the work of another writer. The problem is especially troubling when students *intentionally* take the work of someone else and represent that work as their own. Some schools provide rather rigid and clear-cut policies regarding the punishment for copying someone else's work. It is relatively easy to assign a punishment. The more difficult challenge is in training students to avoid plagiarism, to be sensitive to the need to attribute the work of others, and to gain the confidence to depend on their own efforts.

Focus Questions: As you study the following case, keep these questions in mind: (1) Is there anything positive the teacher can do as the problem *develops* to diminish the impact? (2) What, if anything, should the teacher do to punish the student who you judge to be at fault in this case? (3) What long-term plan can the teacher put in place to help the student who has demonstrated a pattern of dangerous behavior? How can your proposed plan help the teacher to regain a positive emotional climate among the students in her class?

The Case: Copycat

While the other students in her senior honors class worked at their stations in the computer lab, Althea Zelknack shyly approached her teacher, Hilary Inglemeir, and asked in a confidential tone if she could speak to her alone in the hall. "Certainly," responded Hilary, curious to learn the need for Althea's secrecy.

In the hall, speaking in a whisper, Althea confided, "Something happened over the weekend. I didn't know what to do. I told my mom. She said I should talk to you."

Hilary encouraged Althea to continue, expecting but dreading to hear some dark secret about Althea's personal life. Instead, Althea told this story: "On Saturday a few friends were at my house. We were hanging around in my room, talking and listening to music. That morning I had finished a draft of the paper that's due for you next Friday, and I left it next to my computer, on top of the desk. After my friends left, the paper was gone. I thought at first that I misplaced it somewhere. So I thought, 'No big deal. I'll just print another copy.' But I worried a little that if someone had taken the paper from my room and you saw a paper similar to mine, you would think I had copied it. I realized today that someone *did* take my paper. I know who it was."

"I realized today that someone did *take my paper. I know who it was."*

"Who is it?" Hilary whispered.

"It's Wendy Rolfe," claimed Althea.

"How can you be sure it's her?"

"Just now, in the computer lab, I was waiting for my paper to come out of the printer. The paper that came out first, I thought it was mine, but it had Wendy's name on it. I read the first page and it was almost exactly the same as mine. I'm not a confrontational person, and I don't want to accuse Wendy of anything. I just thought you should know, because you'll probably get two papers that are exactly the same."

"Althea, thanks for letting me know. I'll have to wait until the papers are turned in. Maybe Wendy wanted the paper as a model and she won't turn it in as her own. You just turn in your paper as you planned, and don't worry."

While Hilary assured Althea, she had many doubts herself. Through the remainder of the class period, Hilary was distracted by the prospect of dealing with someone who had appropriated someone else's work. Hilary anticipated that in another week she would receive two almost identical papers, and she would have to mete out some sort of punishment to one student for copying. One touchy problem was that Hilary could not prove to anyone that Wendy was the one who had copied the paper. Although Hilary believed Althea, the only evidence for condemning Wendy would be the claim that Althea made against her. Wendy could just as well claim that Althea had copied *her* paper.

Although Hilary believed Althea, the only evidence for condemning Wendy would be the claim that Althea made against her.

That night, Hilary couldn't stop thinking about the problem. She could well imagine Wendy insisting that she had written the paper she would submit in a week. Hilary thought Wendy was a nice young woman, but she was competitive about grades. Hilary couldn't imagine Althea lying to her or copying someone else's paper. The most disturbing aspect of the episode was that one student would intentionally allow her friend to suffer any repercussions that would result when the teacher discovered the plagiarism.

Hilary was hesitant to take any action. She didn't want to accuse Wendy of copying Althea's work when Wendy hadn't yet turned in the assignment. Anticipating the possibility that Wendy would turn in a plagiarized paper, Hilary had to think of an appropriate response. Should she fail Wendy for the assignment and award no credit? Should she reprimand her and allow her to submit a new essay for partial credit? Should she refer Wendy to a dean so that someone else could determine the penalty? Should she contact Wendy's parents to involve them in the punishment and intervention? How would Hilary even prove that it was Wendy who had copied Althea's work and not the other way around? As Hilary tossed and turned in bed, she hoped that Wendy would feel the bite of conscience and ultimately not turn in a plagiarized paper.

During the following week, Hilary noticed a change in the emotional climate of her senior AP class. Wendy's classmates seemed to distance themselves from her. Students avoided joining her for small-group work. She came to class alone and left by herself. She appeared to have no social interaction with the other students. It seemed that the rest of the class had gotten wind of Wendy's indiscretion and determined their own form of punishment. Hilary believed at this point that Wendy would get the message and not submit a plagiarized paper.

Two days before the essay assignment was due, Hilary talked to her colleague Pat Ford, who had had Wendy as a student when Wendy was a sophomore. Pat said, "You know, her parents put a lot of pressure on her to get straight As. Her mom gives her incentives to get good grades—you know, shopping sprees at the mall, that kind of thing. I guess this has been going on for years."

"I'm really concerned," Hilary said. "It seems that all the other kids in her class are mad at her."

"It's no wonder," said Pat. "She's on a mission to become valedictorian at any cost. I heard she dropped her science class because she was afraid she wouldn't get an A. A lot of kids think she's not competing fairly with other students who are candidates for valedictorian because she has fewer classes and an easier schedule."

"I'm afraid," commented Hilary, "that she has developed a pattern that could be disastrous for her future."

On Friday, when all the students turned in their essays, Hilary took the first opportunity to compare the papers of Althea and Wendy. They were almost identical.

Over the weekend, Hilary started grading the papers, but she postponed grading Wendy's and Althea's. She knew she was procrastinating, but she needed more time to think through the problem.

On Monday, Hilary arrived early at school and passed Wendy's locker on her way to her classroom. She noticed two poems taped to the locker—one, cut from the comic strip section of the Sunday newspaper, was written by children's book author Jack Prelutsky; the other was a handwritten parody of the Prelutsky poem. The handwritten version, apparently intended to mock Wendy, read as follows:

> Oh Essays, Oh Essays,
> I hate you, you stink.
> I wish I could stick you down in a sink.
> Oh Essays, Oh Essays,
> You're giving me fits.
> I'm sick to my stomach and have
> a case of the sh_ _ s!
>
> I'd rather go to prom with
> a bumbling dork
> Than write my own essay,
> an original work.
> I don't like you Essays,
> I hate you so much.
> And I really hate school;
> I think that it sucks.
>
> I don't want to go here,
> But I must get straight A's!
> So I'll copy all day
> And I'll copy all night.
> At least this one has no copyright!

Hilary knew that the poems were meant to attack and hurt Wendy, so she removed them from her locker. In the teachers' workroom, Hilary saw Pat Ford and showed her the two poems.

"Oh, my God," said Pat. "This Prelutsky poem is the one that Wendy submitted as her own for our class poetry anthology in sophomore English. I remember because everyone liked it, and Wendy got a lot of attention for being clever enough to invent it. Some kid must have seen it in the paper this weekend and made the connection. It's too bad that Wendy feels she has to do this kind of thing. Her classmates are certainly on to her. I wouldn't want to be in Wendy's shoes for anything."

Hilary knew that the poems were meant to attack and hurt Wendy, so she removed them from her locker. In the teachers' workroom, Hilary saw Pat Ford and showed her the two poems.

Hilary groaned. This seemed to be corroborating evidence to prove that Wendy rather than Althea had copied the paper. Hilary had something tangible with which to confront Wendy. Hilary knew she couldn't hold on to the papers forever. She would have to decide how to contend with Wendy and how she would treat Althea. **If you were in Hilary's position, what would you do?**

Questions for Discussion

1. What substantive evidence, if any, does Hilary have that it was Wendy who plagiarized? How can you judge if the evidence is sufficient for Hilary to move forward with some disciplinary action toward Wendy?
2. If Hilary judges that it was Wendy who plagiarized, how could she adequately demonstrate to Wendy and her parents that Wendy has done something seriously wrong? How will Wendy and her parents likely react? Given the parents' probable reaction, how can Hilary proceed without getting into a contentious debate?
3. Should Hilary punish Wendy? How have you arrived at your judgment? If punishment is appropriate, what form should the punishment take?
4. To what extent does Hilary have a responsibility to protect Wendy's emotional state? What, if anything, can she do?
5. What actions should Hilary take in the near term and in the long run?
6. Should Hilary have acted sooner? What, if anything, could she have done?
7. What policies and/or procedures can Hilary put in place for the future so that similar episodes do not occur again?

Related Research and Writing

Select one of the following areas of investigation, research the topic, and produce a brief written report that you can share with your colleagues.

1. Find out the policy regarding plagiarism at a school with which you are familiar. How is *plagiarism* defined? How are students taught about plagiarism and how to avoid it? What penalty do students face if they are caught plagiarizing? Do individual teachers have the discretion to decide how to respond to each case? What changes would you make to improve the school's policy?
2. Discuss with another teacher experiences they have had with students who have copied the work of other students or of published writers. What

were the circumstances (e.g., the specific assignment, the time of year, the student's age, etc.)? How did the teacher treat the student? How did the student respond? Beyond assigning any penalty, what did the teacher do to try to discourage the student from repeating the same behavior in the future?

3. Examine several style manuals, handbooks, and curriculum guides to read a variety of policy statements about plagiarism. Then devise a statement of your own. Have in mind students of a particular age. How will you define *plagiarism*? How can you model for students some reliable ways to avoid inadvertently plagiarizing? Share your written statement with your colleagues and solicit suggestions for revisions.

12 To Think or Not to Think, That Is the Question

Preview: It is a myth that teaching honors students is easy. They are smart and sophisticated, and they present few behavior problems. But when the curriculum calls for teaching students critical thinking and problem-solving skills and to learn how to interpret literature, the task can be difficult even for the more advanced students. The teacher in this case is confronted with circumstances that nearly every teacher must deal with at one point or another: Why won't this group of supposedly well-equipped honors students think critically? Her attempts to get them to work cooperatively, to discuss and debate important issues and themes raised in the literature, and to interpret the literature they are reading are frustrated at every turn. This case brings into focus some of the problems and issues that English teachers must contend with when attempting to teach students higher-order thinking skills.

Focus Questions: As you study this case, consider the following questions: (1) Should the teacher keep trying to get her students to learn and practice critical thinking and problem-solving skills that are important for students in honors and AP classes? If she decides to continue trying, how should she proceed? (2) To what extent does the teacher contribute to the problems she is having in getting her students to think critically? What can she do to overcome these problems?

The Case: To Think or Not to Think, That Is the Question

Julie Benvolio was thrilled when she was told that one of the courses she was going to teach at John C. Fremont Memorial High School was tenth-grade honors English. She was especially pleased because she had heard that first-year teachers were rarely assigned honors students. When she raised concerns about her lack of teaching experience to the department chair, Carlos Sanchez, he dismissed them with a wave of his hand and assured her that he thought she had excellent credentials and could do a good job. In fact, he said that one of the ninth-grade honors teachers described this particular group of students as "real go-getters," so she shouldn't have any problems. He told her that if she did have any questions or problems, she should feel free to talk with any of the other honors teachers, or he would be more than happy to help her out.

When Julie met a few days before school started with the two other teachers who taught the course, the course leader, Koji Kagawa, pointed out how important it was to emphasize critical thinking and problem solving in their teaching. "After all," he said, "these kids are honors students. Our goal is to make them independent thinkers and problem solvers. Remember," he added, "part of our job is to get them ready for the kind of critical thinking that will be required of them in the next couple of years when they will be taking the AP exams."

Julie would ask a question and then find herself looking out at a sea of puzzled eyes staring back at her, the students sitting quietly, with their notebooks opened in front of them, pencils in hand, waiting to write down her every word.

The first few days of school Julie was pleased with how nice the honors students seemed. However, she had to admit that the department chair's description of the students as "go-getters" was almost comical. They came to class with sharpened pencils, and if Julie made a comment about the weather, they would immediately write it down in their notebooks and ask whether her comment would be on a test. Her first couple of attempts to hold class discussions were dismal failures. Julie would ask a question and then find herself looking out at a sea of puzzled eyes staring back at her, the students sitting quietly, with their notebooks opened in front of them, pencils in hand, waiting to write down her every word. Despite vowing to have the students do the thinking and talking, she found herself answering most of her own questions. The students did fine when answering literal questions, but as soon as she asked a question that required real thinking, the room suddenly became deadly silent until she relented and answered the question herself.

The results of her first few homework assignments and quiz were also disappointing. Although they were all turned in on time, the students' written answers to questions were most often short and literal. On the first quiz, many of the students earned a grade of C. When Julie handed them back, she got lots of complaints. Some of the students argued that the quiz had been too hard, and Mark, who seemed to speak for most of the students in the class, complained that he didn't see how they could be expected to know the answer to at least one of the hard questions because she "hadn't gone over it in class."

The situation finally came to a head a little over a month into the school year, just after the class had taken its first unit test and Julie had assigned them to read Kate Chopin's short story "A Pair of Silk Stockings."

"Are the tests graded yet, Ms. Benvolio?" Dave spoke politely as he and Aleksander dashed through the classroom door.

"Yeah, how'd we do?" asked Aleksander as they both walked up to her desk.

Julie replied, "Yes, yes, they're graded, but first we are going to examine that short story I asked you to read. So take your seats, guys, okay?"

As the two boys turned around, they noticed the arrangement of desks in the room. "Oh, no, not again," groaned Dave under his breath.

She purposely had put the desks in small groups before class because she didn't want to give students a chance to get settled into their much preferred routine of taking notes while she talked.

Sophia, one of the more gifted students in the class, and some of the other students were now entering the room. "Don't make us work in groups again, Ms. Benvolio," Sophia moaned. "That wasn't fair last time when you gave us group grades. I mean, I did most of the work."

Julie knew that this period was not going to be easy. She purposely had put the desks in small groups before class because she didn't want to give students a chance to get settled into their much preferred routine of taking notes while she talked.

"Take any open seat you can find for now, class; once I take attendance and explain the activity I want you to do, I'll put you in the small groups I've assigned you to. I have your unit tests from yesterday, but I'll return them at the end of class so we can focus on the activity I want you to do with the story."

"Could you please at least give us our test scores now?" begged Ann. A chorus of voices joined in.

"How many got As?"

"What was the top score?"

"What was the average grade?"

"Please, class, not now. I said later. Everyone did fine, so relax. But I think everyone in this class can benefit from practice that will force you to consider other opinions and to discuss different interpretations. So we're going to work together today, in small groups, to do just that. Listen up for your name and the group I have assigned you to."

After the students got into their groups, Julie passed out the questions she wanted them to work on and announced, "Look carefully at the questions I have given you. Most of them ask for an interpretation. That is, the answers are not directly stated in the text. I want you to discuss and debate the questions as a group and come up with a group answer. I want one person to be the recorder and write down what the group decides. When you are done, we will discuss your answers as a class. Does everyone understand what I want you to do? Okay, then, get started."

Julie stood back to let the groups work on their own for a while, and then she began circulating among the groups to check on their progress. She was dismayed with what she found. As she approached the group nearest the front of the room, she quickly discerned that no one was doing the assignment: two boys were discussing what they were going to do Friday night, one girl was covertly doing a homework assignment for her science class that was due next period, and another girl was just staring at the questions for the short story. Julie reprimanded the group and, after some further prompting, got them discussing the questions.

When she approached another group, she discovered that the entire group had let one girl answer all the questions for everyone. As she approached a third group, she saw one boy quickly shove his phone in the front of his hoodie, and the rest of the group sat silently listening while two boys debated the answer to one of the questions. Julie encouraged other students in the group to speak up and express their views, and she moved on when it was clear that this group was finally involved in a group discussion. The last group appeared to be discussing something, but as she got closer, she discovered that two girls were discussing a writing assignment for their journalism class, another girl was writing out the answers to the short story questions, while the rest of the group sat quietly doing nothing. After some coaxing and cajoling, she finally got this group on task.

When she approached another group, she discovered that the entire group had let one girl answer all the questions for everyone.

When Julie looked up at the clock, she realized there were only a few minutes left in the period; it had taken most of the period to get the groups doing what she wanted them to do. She also knew there wouldn't be enough time to go over the group answers. Just when she was about to make an announcement, Sophia interrupted her to ask if they would be graded on their group work. Before she could formulate a response, a chorus of student voices began complaining about group grades.

When she got the class quiet, Julie told them they would finish up their small-group discussions tomorrow and discuss their answers with the whole class. Then she returned their tests and began reviewing one of the inferential questions a number of students had had trouble answering. "Can someone tell us how they answered the question about 'Leningen versus the Ants'? 'Do the events of the story support Leningen's lifelong motto, or do they reveal that it is not necessarily true? Explain.'" Julie looked around the room for volunteers but saw, from the expressions on students' faces, that she might easily wait until sometime next week.

"Okay, then, listen," Julie began, and proceeded to offer them one possible interpretation in the hope that it might prompt them to give another possible interpretation. Julie was finishing her response and turning it into a question—"So that is how the events in the story support his lifelong motto. But how might the events reveal that the motto is maybe not true? Could someone answer . . .?"—when a student interrupted before Julie could finish.

"So, if it's just your opinion, then one answer is as good as another!" someone said. "Anybody who has a reasonable answer ought to get credit!"

"Yeah! Everyone should get credit for an answer!" others said.

The bell rang before Julie could respond, and six or seven students started lining up at her desk as the rest gathered up their books and materials and headed for the door. As the line of students asking for extra points was forming, Julie wondered if there was anything she could do to get her students to think critically. **If you were in Julie's situation, what would you do?**

Questions for Discussion

1. How can teachers help their students understand the importance of learning and practicing critical thinking and problem-solving techniques in English classes?
2. To what extent is emphasizing individual grades and test points detrimental to the process of helping students learn critical thinking and problem-solving techniques?
3. Since the course is designed to prepare students for the Advanced Placement English examinations, which are graded individually, is it fair to students to encourage them to work in groups during their English class? Why or why not?
4. To what extent is it fair and reasonable for Julie to assign students group grades?
5. To what extent is having students work in small groups helping them to learn critical thinking and problem-solving strategies?
6. Why do you think Julie is having so much trouble getting this group of students to think critically?

7. Some might argue that getting this group of students to think is a hopeless task. Do you agree? Why or why not? Is there anything wrong with emphasizing objective information that students can recall? Explain.
8. What possible courses of action does Julie have at this point? For example, where else can she turn for help? What might she do in class tomorrow? How might this help to solve the problem?
9. What is the best course of action for Julie? Why do you think that is the best course of action for her to take?
10. What lessons can be learned from this case? For example, to what extent should all students be learning critical thinking and problem-solving skills in English class?

Related Research and Writing

Select one of the following areas of investigation, research the topic, and produce a brief written or oral report that you can share with other students in your class or with your colleagues.

1. Read an article, book, or monograph about approaches to teaching higher-order thinking. Here are a few possibilities: Thomas M. McCann et al.'s *Reflective Teaching, Reflective Learning*; Jeffrey D. Wilhelm's *Engaging Readers and Writers with Inquiry*; or Elizabeth A. Kahn et al.'s *Inquiry Paths to Literacy Learning*. What are the strengths and weaknesses of these approaches? Which approach do you think would be most effective? Why?
2. Talk to veteran teachers about challenges they have had teaching honors-level classes. What are the major challenges? How do they address these challenges?
3. Read a book or monograph about different approaches to teaching critical thinking and interpreting literature, such as Larry R. Johannessen, Elizabeth A. Kahn, and Carolyn Calhoun Walter's *Writing about Literature,* 2nd Edition; Richard Beach et al.'s *Teaching Literature to Adolescents*; or Deborah Appleman's *Critical Encounters in Secondary English.* What are the strengths and weaknesses of the approach? How would you use these materials in your own teaching? Create an activity for a work of literature you are teaching based on ideas from the book.
4. Examine a book or monograph like Jacqueline Darvin's *Teaching the Tough Issues Classes* or Antero Garcia and Cindy O'Donnell-Allen's *Pose, Wobble, Flow,* which introduces methods intended to help teachers address difficult

or controversial topics in the classroom. What are the strengths and weaknesses of the approach? How would you use these materials in your own teaching?

13

Call Me Irreplaceable

Preview: It is difficult for a new teacher to replace a popular teacher. The replacement will naturally be tempted to follow some of the practices that made their predecessor popular. It is understandable that a teacher will want to be liked by students and parents. Popularity sometimes comes at a price, however, when a teacher cannot find their own identity. In the following case, a new teacher follows a legend. While the new teacher would like to emulate some of the finer qualities of the veteran teacher, she knows it is impossible to do everything just the way the older teacher did.

Focus Questions: As you study the case, consider the following questions: (1) Should the teacher attempt to please students and parents? (2) Is it possible to satisfy students and parents yet lose the confidence of colleagues? Whose judgment and sentiments should guide the teacher?

The Case: Call Me Irreplaceable

At Eleanor Keeneway's retirement party, Stan Lofton, the principal of Gresham Middle School, described her as "irreplaceable" and a "monument to middle school teaching." Parents, former students, and colleagues tearfully recalled special moments in the career of Mrs. Keeneway. Parents and students loved her kindness and her patience. She seemed to take a personal interest in each child.

Colleagues had the impression that Eleanor Keeneway somehow found the time to attend each music performance, athletic event, social function, and fundraising activity in which her students were involved. Parents shared with one another the belief that students who had struggled academically with other teachers thrived in seventh grade under Mrs. Keeneway. Mr. Lofton could recall no parent complaint about Mrs. Keeneway during his ten-year tenure as principal at Gresham.

When Mr. Lofton hired Ann Kobitz to replace Mrs. Keeneway, he warned her that she would be "filling some mighty big shoes." As a young first-year teacher, recently graduated from college, Ann was a bit intimidated by the challenge of replacing the "irreplaceable." She only hoped that everyone would give her time to adjust and not expect her to become a second Mrs. Keeneway.

At the beginning of the school year, Ann worked diligently to live up to what she believed was the Keeneway standard. She devoted hours to planning purposeful lessons, grading papers, and offering students substantial feedback on their work. She believed that she embraced realistic learning expectations, which she explicitly shared with her students. Ann attempted to make appearances at as many student activities as possible, but she prioritized her planning and assessment before her attendance at school activities.

By the middle of October, Ann began to feel the strain of attempting to provide purposeful and engaging lessons, read and respond to her students' frequent writing, and support students in their athletic, artistic, social, and emotional development.

By the middle of October, Ann began to feel the strain of attempting to provide purposeful and engaging lessons, read and respond to her students' frequent writing, and support students in their athletic, artistic, social, and emotional development. There were times when Ann chose to meet family obligations or visit with friends rather than attend another soccer game or choral concert. Soon Ann began to hear some grumbling among her students and a few complaints from parents. Students asked, "Why weren't you at the cross-country meet last night?" or "Why do we have so much homework?" One parent phone call resonated in Ann's memory. The parent said, "I've had three kids who went through seventh grade with Mrs. Keeneway, and they never received this much work or such poor grades." Even the librarian was critical of a complex research project that required the students to work in the learning center for four days and collaborate in teams of two or three. The librarian sniffed, "Mrs. Keeneway never would have done things this way."

In contrast, Mrs. Keeneway was not nearly as popular among the two eighth-grade language arts teachers. Jack Docent observed, "I won't deny that the kids loved Eleanor, but I don't think she taught them anything about writing. She made the kids feel good about themselves, but she really didn't demand much. And Eleanor would be the first to admit that her primary concern was with protecting the kids' psyches. She saw middle school as a time for kids to grow up with their personalities intact. She was less concerned about attending to goals for reading and writing." Leslie Ward complained, "She made our job much more difficult because a lot of kids coasted for a year and now have to do some work and learn to write. You can easily tell the difference between those students who had Mrs. Keeneway last year and those who had another teacher. We have to field complaints from parents because students are struggling now after they had great grades last year. Eleanor really put us in a vulnerable position. I really like Eleanor as a person, but I'm glad you have replaced her. It will make my job a lot easier."

At the back of one file drawer in the room that Ann inherited, she found stacks of ungraded papers and wondered if Mrs. Keeneway had ever read them.

Ann made casual discoveries about the nature of Mrs. Keeneway's instruction. At the back of one file drawer in the room that Ann inherited, she found stacks of ungraded papers and wondered if Mrs. Keeneway had ever read them. The media specialist at Gresham assured Ann that her classroom technology was in great working order and asked if Ann wanted to rely on the same streaming services that Mrs. Keeneway always used. An eighth-grade sibling of one of Ann's current students noted, "We never got homework last year. Mrs. Keeneway brought us doughnuts every Friday. She made learning fun. She was really cool."

Ann knew that she could not become a clone of Mrs. Keeneway. She soon realized that she could not be at every school event and keep close track of every child. At the same time, Ann wanted students and parents to like her. She also realized that as a nontenured teacher she would be vulnerable if parents started complaining about her to the principal, who appeared to have been Mrs. Keeneway's biggest fan.

In some ways, Ann felt like a victim of fraud. She was now the target of criticism because her predecessor had pandered to children and parents. Ann's first response was anger; she felt like exposing Eleanor Keeneway as an incompetent who had essentially retired on the job. Ann thought that people should know, after all, what Mrs. Keeneway was really like as a classroom instructor. Of course, attacking the popular legend would have its dangers.

Ann also considered rethinking her instructional approach so that her performance standards weren't so high and her homework assignments were fewer and less involved. She knew that if she were more liberal with grades and homework, there would be fewer parent complaints, which would make a more favorable impression on the principal, who was her immediate supervisor.

With approximately a month before the parent-teacher conferences that were scheduled on the days before Thanksgiving, Ann knew she would have to make some adjustments before she met with parents. She knew she couldn't be Mrs. Keeneway, so who could she be? **If you were in Ann's position, what adjustments, if any, would you make in the next month?**

Questions for Discussion

1. To what extent should Ann follow the example set by Mrs. Keeneway? To what extent should she worry about pleasing her students and their parents? If she makes changes, how should she handle the complaints?
2. What are the many pressures that Ann faces as she defines her instruction and her teacher practices? Which pressures, if any, must she respond to?
3. Ann's eighth-grade colleagues expect her to improve on Mrs. Keeneway's efforts to prepare students to meet the expectations of the next grade. How fair and realistic are these expectations?
4. To what extent does Ann need to pattern herself after Mrs. Keeneway to satisfy her principal and get a good evaluation?

Related Research and Writing

Select one of the following areas of investigation, research the topic, and produce a brief written or oral report that you can share with other students in your class or your colleagues.

1. View or recall several movies that depict the behavior of classroom teachers (e.g., *Dead Poets Society, Lean on Me, Stand and Deliver, Dangerous Minds, Freedom Writers*). How do these films represent teachers? To what extent do the images stand up to your experiences and your vision of a good teacher? Consider the ways in which such films might influence society's expectations of teachers and thereby set an unrealistic standard for a new teacher. Where, if anywhere, do you see problems between popular media images and the actual reality of working in the classroom?
2. Talk to a few students of various ages and ask them who their favorite teachers are. What do they like about these teachers? Are there some common attributes among the favorites? Do the attributes represent characteristics that you aspire to as a teacher? Share your findings and observations with your classmates or colleagues.
3. Recall a teacher you remember fondly and who had a positive influence on your life and your learning. What were the qualities you liked in this teacher? To what extent are you able to emulate this person you admire? Is it realistic to think that you could be anything like the person who made such a positive impression on you? Share your story and insights with your classmates or colleagues.

14

Evening Reveries

Preview: When teachers genuinely care about their students, they experience some emotionally wrenching situations. The teacher in the following case believes that he has encountered too many troubling stories, and he seeks relief, perhaps by leaving the teaching profession altogether. Is it possible to prepare for the emotional toll that comes from learning about the lives of your students? Is it possible, and advisable, to try to work only in schools where students seem to be relatively free of problems? If teachers feel an obligation to help others, should they seek to help where students are the neediest?

Focus Questions: As you study the following case, consider these questions: (1) To what extent is the teacher in this case facing a situation that is typical for most teachers? Will the current impact of the problems diminish over time? (2) What actions should the teacher take to help himself cope with the current school year? What should he do about his future in teaching?

The Case: Evening Reveries

Wade Rivers slowly climbed the back stairs to his apartment after school on a gray Friday afternoon in February. Wade was usually tired on Friday afternoon, but today he felt completely drained. After entering his apartment, he dropped his backpack inside the door, shuffled to the living room, and flopped onto the couch. It was as if someone had pulled an electrical plug and cut off his energy supply. He had nothing left.

Wade fell into a deep sleep as the sun set and the room darkened. Two hours later he woke up to the sound of his phone. He picked it up off the arm of the couch: it was a group text.

Kenny: "Where RU???"

Chris: "Don't make us late we're waiting on you."

Janel: "He's always late these days. What's up with him? I'm not coming over. I'll just see you all there."

Chris: "Wadddeeeee COME ON."

Wade rubbed his eyes. It was seven-thirty. He was supposed to meet at Chris's place before going to the game.

Wade: "Fell asleep after school. Go without me."

He tossed the phone to the other end of the couch. He wanted to go to the game, but realistically he had no energy to do anything but sleep. He got up, turned off the lights, and went into his bedroom.

Clearly, the week at Pasteur Metro High School had taken an emotional toll on Wade.

Wade assumed that he would just immediately drift into a deep sleep. Instead, he tossed and turned. He couldn't help but review the events of the week at school. He couldn't stop thinking about recent revelations about some of his students. Clearly, the week at Pasteur Metro High School had taken an emotional toll on Wade. He abandoned for now the hope that he would soon fall asleep and sat up to reach for the TV remote.

As Wade scrolled through the new releases on his favorite streaming service, he picked an episode of a popular spy series. But it quickly faded into the background as he began to inventory the disturbing experiences from the week. On Monday, Wade had spoken to the school's social worker about Letty, a ninth grader whose frequent absences and apparently chronic fatigue disturbed Wade. The social worker confided that she believed the girl's mother had introduced her to, and more or less forced her to participate in, prostitution. Wade was outraged at the report and wanted the mother arrested, but the social worker noted that she had no substantive evidence to support her intuitions. The idea of a student forced into prostitution was shocking to Wade. He considered this student to still be a little girl, and it was outrageous that someone in her own family was willing to put her life at risk to make money.

An officer told Wade to "keep out of it" when Wade tried to intervene. It was a terrifying incident that left him shaken and feeling powerless to advocate for his students.

On Tuesday, Wade saw three of his students detained by police officers who were in the process of going through the boys' bags as Wade approached. One of the boys, Andre, told Wade that they had been walking home after basketball practice. Seems their one mistake was taking up the bike lane along the street and not using the sidewalk. An officer told Wade to "keep out of it" when Wade tried to intervene. It was a terrifying incident that left him shaken and feeling powerless to advocate for his students.

Twenty minutes passed, and a pause before the next episode of the program started snapped Wade from his reverie. He realized that he couldn't remember anything he had just watched. His mind was deep in worry for his students.

Wade chose a different show, one far more mindless, and his thoughts turned to reflections about another student. Wade had learned through a counselor that Atalanta, another ninth grader, would soon be leaving with her family for Mexico. Atalanta was fighting leukemia. The family had tried several conventional medical treatments, with no success. When doctors predicted that Atalanta would soon die, the family sought help at a clinic in Mexico, where they would have access to medications that had not been approved by the FDA in the United States. The Atalanta's family took out a second mortgage on their modest home, started a HelpFundUs page, and sold many possessions to raise the money for the trip and treatment in Mexico. Wade did not share the family's hopeful outlook. He felt certain that this gentle young student would not survive, and the family would return deeper in debt.

If he delved at all into the personal lives of his students, he was confronted by an array of demons—teenage pregnancies, substance abuse, child abuse and neglect, police violence, poverty, fear and desperation.

Wade paused the show. He recognized that he couldn't help but bring home with him the daily stories of his students' misery, hardship, or catastrophe. This week's happenings in the troubled lives of Letty, Andre, and Atalanta were simply the latest installments in the continuous cavalcade of grief and hardship that Wade witnessed at Pasteur Metro High. If he delved at all into the personal lives of his students, he was confronted by an array of demons—teenage pregnancies, substance abuse, child abuse and neglect, police violence, poverty, fear and desperation.

Whenever Wade learned that one of his students was having a problem, he tried to step in. He contacted the social worker, the counselor, the dean, the nurse, the police, the parents—anyone to find help for a troubled child. He learned quickly that most problems were complex, and his efforts to help were usually futile. He felt helpless, yet he worried about each child. The worry and disappointment were clearly taking an emotional toll. When Wade could objectively distance himself from events, he could recognize that his work was important, and he could recall many success stories at Pasteur Metro High. But in light of recent events, he could only dwell on the negative.

Here at the end of the week, Wade thought, "That's it. I'm not asking any more questions. It doesn't pay to learn about the personal lives of these kids. I can't help, and I just suffer with them. Ignorance may not be bliss, but ignorance might help me to cope."

It was clear that if he continued to work in the same place with the same approach, he would eventually experience some sort of breakdown.

Wade had graduated from a teacher education program that was committed to preparing teachers for work in urban education. He had grown up in an affluent white suburb but was attracted by the racial and economic diversity of the city, characteristics he saw as strengths rather than drawbacks, unlike some of his colleagues. Wade felt a sense of mission in working in a school in the core of the city. He believed that the city's public high schools had long been neglected and needed the commitment of dedicated young teachers.

Wade turned off the TV. He thought maybe he could now sleep, as he had come to one piece of a larger decision: he couldn't continue to absorb the repeated emotional shocks that were an inevitable part of life at Pasteur Metro High School. Wade knew he had to make a change, but he wondered what he could do. It was clear that if he continued to work in the same place with the same approach, he would eventually experience some sort of breakdown.

Life at Pasteur High was tough. It was part of a big urban school system where the complicated bureaucracy slowed action and made it difficult to get things done, even basics like getting books and supplies. The system made many demands on teachers to prepare students for various standardized tests that were intended to hold teachers and local administrators accountable for students' performances. Most of the students lacked motivation and came to high school woefully deficient in basic academic skills. Working at Pasteur was a challenge, and Wade concluded that knowing about the lives of his students and caring deeply about them was making his work tougher rather than easier.

Wade repositioned his pillow and put his head back for another attempt at sleep. As he stared at the ceiling, hearing the muffled traffic noise from the street below his window and feeling the lonely crush of the consuming darkness, he believed that he had only two options if he were to continue teaching. He could shut himself off from any of the personal aspects of his students' lives, which would mean concerning himself only with the life within his classroom and expecting students to leave their troubles at the doorstep. He thought also about leaving Pasteur and finding a job in a less challenging school in a wealthy suburb. One of his college classmates was already working at Bonnybrook Valley High School. His old friend had told Wade there would be an opening there next year. This teacher also reported that administrators at BVHS had high regard for graduates of their college, so he was likely to be hired if he applied.

Wade wondered whether he could really escape to a school where students had few serious problems, at least less serious than the ones he encountered at

Pasteur. He also felt the pinch of conscience because he would be turning his back on his mission and abandoning those students who were in the greatest need of his services and talents. Wade wondered if he could realistically continue to work at Pasteur but ignore the troubling personal affairs of his students. Perhaps with experience he would become a bit more callused so that each trial and tragedy didn't carry an emotional burden. **What should Wade do?**

Questions for Discussion

1. Is it necessary that Wade know something about the personal lives of his students to serve them as their teacher? Explain. Is it possible for him to remain aloof and ignorant of students' troubles? Explain.
2. Difficulties look especially grim in the middle of the night when a person is fatigued from a tough week of work. To what extent might Wade be exaggerating the difficulties he is exposed to? Are the problems likely to appear less significant to Wade the next day, after he is rested? Explain.
3. Is there anyone to whom Wade could turn for help? Who could he talk to? Would his college classmate at the suburban high school help? Is there someone at Pasteur Metro High who could help? How could conversation with someone else be of any use to Wade?
4. Do you agree with Wade that he has an obligation or mission to serve students who live in a troubled environment? Why would he define this mission for himself? Does his rationale make any sense?
5. What short-term and long-term solutions can you devise for Wade? Imagine that you had to present Wade with some options. What rationale can you provide to support a particular course of action?
6. What hope is there for schools like Pasteur Metro High? Do the best and brightest teachers at such schools inevitably get frustrated and abandon the schools? What supports should be available to encourage talented teachers to stay?

Related Research and Writing

Select one of the following areas of investigation, research the topic, and produce a brief oral or written report that you can share with your classmates or colleagues.

1. Talk to a veteran teacher about their views on the importance of knowing as much as possible about the lives of their students. How does the teacher

learn about the students? How does information about their lives help the teacher with instructional planning? To what extent does the teacher attempt to intervene when they see a need for help? To what extent does the teacher find that having knowledge about students' personal lives is emotionally taxing?

2. Read current reports about the state of high schools in the United States. What are the trends? How are schools being made safer? Are there significant disparities in the kinds of troubles students face when urban and suburban schools are compared? Are there disparities in which students are disciplined and how they are disciplined? Since all high schools enroll adolescents, the students will experience the inevitable challenges of negotiating the dangerous ground between childhood and adulthood. Where do you see evidence that some schools have students who face egregious difficulties? Is there any way to predict which schools will have the most trouble?

15

When Do They Do Grammar?

Preview: It is not uncommon for someone to meet an English teacher and say, "Oh, I'd better watch my grammar!" The comment reveals a stereotype of English teachers as sensitive to the strict adherence to rules of a standard way of speaking and writing, teachers who will publicly admonish those who violate the rules. The image also suggests that much of what English teachers do in the classroom is drill students on grammar rules, have them parse sentences, and expect them to express themselves "correctly." In actuality, it's more likely that English language arts teachers will eschew the drill in grammar and focus instruction on the writing process. A few critics, however, have wondered if this shift in emphasis has been a good one. In their enthusiasm for process-oriented methods for teaching writing, have teachers neglected instruction in grammar? Should grammar instruction be a cornerstone of the English language arts curriculum?

Focus Questions: As you study the following case, keep these questions in mind: (1) Are both the new teacher and the veteran teacher correct in their approach to English instruction? How can they both be right? (2) Would you agree that there is substantial evidence that the approach of the veteran teacher is an effective one for the teaching of English? (3) What different conceptions of language arts instruction do the new teacher and the veteran teacher represent?

The Case: When Do They Do Grammar?

During parent-teacher conferences in November, the mother of Grant Stuma asked her daughter's eighth-grade English teacher, "Is Grant supposed to be bringing home a grammar book? The only thing I see her bringing home is a paperback novel. When my son Nathan was in Mr. Boswell's eighth-grade classroom, he brought home his grammar book and had homework every night. He had to learn the rules for correct grammar. Some of the homework even involved diagramming sentences. It was hard at first, but he got the hang of it and thought it was fun—sort of a puzzle. When do kids do grammar in your class?"

Monique Howard, in her first year of teaching at St. Procopius School, attempted a summary description of her approach to teaching language and writing: "You see, Ms. Stuma, we study grammar and usage and mechanics as part of the editing stage of the writing process. I am most interested in teaching students how to *write*, and research in the teaching of writing shows us that drill in grammar doesn't really help students learn to write. So I don't have students do exercises out of a grammar text, but we do study grammar as necessary when we are editing our writing. I find very short lessons focusing on a grammatical structure they can use right away in that writing assignment is the best way to improve their writing. I'm most concerned at this point with the students' writing *fluency*, and I believe that their grammatical correctness will develop over time."

"I don't know, " said Ms. Stuma, skeptically. "My son has turned into a pretty good writer."

"I don't doubt that Nathan is a good writer," responded Monique, "but I plan to teach writing as a thinking process, and I will focus on grammar and usage as a part of the process."

"I just hope," concluded Ms. Stuma, "that Grant will be ready for high school. I don't pretend to know the latest trends in teaching English. All I know is that when I was in seventh and eighth grade, we did a lot of work in grammar, and that work helped me a lot in high school. Knowing grammar was a big advantage when I learned a foreign language, and I became a pretty good writer. I don't mean that I'm some F. Scott Fitzgerald or something, but I remember getting good grades on essays and compositions in high school."

"All I know is that when I was in seventh and eighth grade we did a lot of work in grammar, and that work helped me a lot in high school."

Monique thanked Ms. Stuma for sharing her observations about the teaching of grammar and tried to reassure her that she would not neglect her daughter's preparation for high school. After the conference, Monique reflected on Ms. Stuma's remarks. As a graduate of St. Procopius School herself, Monique had anticipated some conservative views among the faculty and parents. When she began teaching at the school, she was confident that her approach to the teaching of writing, which did not rely on the study of grammar as the focus, was the right direction to take. She would just have to demonstrate over time that her approach was effective. It would take some time to educate the parents and prove that her approach had some merit.

Ms. Stuma's comments were not the first testimonial that Monique had heard in favor of Mr. Boswell's traditional approach to teaching grammar in his English class—parents, students, and other teachers had loudly sung the praises of Mr. Boswell. Franny Pastorelli, one of Monique's colleagues, noted: "You know, Monique, everyone says that Tom Boswell's students always do well on the standardized tests. I know that the achievement tests don't reveal everything about what students have learned, but he has a reputation for being good at preparing students for the tests." Monique had to admit that this was true. Furthermore, she was aware that last year, two of Tom Boswell's students had won the Writing Achievement Awards that were sponsored by the State Association for Teachers of English (SATE). The competition for the awards required students to produce compositions under timed circumstances. Many people believed Mr. Boswell to be an expert in teaching English. Apparently, Mr. Boswell's students could do more than just fill in bubbles on a computer screen or multiple-choice answer sheet. Parents were pleased that students who had Tom Boswell for English were sufficiently prepared to study grammar in the world language classes they took in high school.

When she began teaching at the school, she was confident that her approach to the teaching of writing, which did not rely on the study of grammar as the focus, was the right direction to take.

After hearing many testimonials in favor of Mr. Boswell's approach to the teaching of English, Monique began to become somewhat resentful, because she equated the praise for him with some vague, implied criticism of her. At the same time, she found it impossible to resent Tom Boswell himself. He was a warm, compassionate, and generous person. Many students liked him because he took personal interest in each one; he was positive and supportive. When Monique started teaching at St. Procopius, Tom was quick to introduce himself and assure her that he was always available to assist her. He offered to share with Monique any of the instructional materials he used, but the material always seemed to be quite different from the emphasis and style that Monique had chosen for her own classroom.

After hearing many testimonials in favor of Mr. Boswell's approach to the teaching of English, Monique began to become somewhat resentful, because she equated the praise for him with some vague, implied criticism of her.

Monique also recognized that Tom Boswell was not old-fashioned and narrow-minded. He was a member of professional organizations for teachers of English. He attended conferences and read the journals to stay current in the teaching of English. In fact, he had published articles himself and had presented sessions at conferences. In general, colleagues from outside the school viewed him as a conscientious, reliable, and creative teacher. In school, everyone seemed to defer to the learned and erudite Mr. Boswell at meetings when issues about curriculum and instruction were discussed.

Students also held Mr. Boswell in high regard. They liked his class because they liked *him*. Students regarded his lessons as "fun." Indeed, Monique could see that he used a variety of games and cooperative learning structures as a means for teaching grammar. Sometimes Monique's own students would ask, "Why do we have to *write* all the time? Why can't we do some fun stuff like they do in Mr. Boswell's class?"

In the face of the many testimonials for Tom Boswell's approach and in light of his reputation as an effective teacher, Monique began to have some concerns that perhaps *she* was the one who was out of step with best practices in the teaching of English. Upon leaving the university where she was prepared in the teaching of English, with special emphasis on the teaching of writing, Monique felt supremely confident that she knew exactly the right approach to language arts instruction. Now, however, when she was a practitioner in a school with other competent English teachers who had other reasonable approaches to teaching English, Monique's confidence was shaken. She wondered if the time-tested practices sponsored by many English teachers and by parents were better. She questioned whether she should rethink the emphasis in her English class and pay more attention to direct instruction in grammar. After all, the emphasis on grammar seemed to be working for Mr. Boswell. **If you were in Monique's position, would you change your approach to the teaching of English and place greater emphasis on the teaching of grammar?**

Questions for Discussion

1. Some observers might believe that Mr. Boswell's approach to instruction is more effective than Monique's. What evidence, if any, is there to support this conclusion?
2. If the practices in Mr. Boswell's class run counter to the training that Monique received at the university, should she dismiss his approach as antiquated and ineffective? How can Monique determine what the right approach is?
3. On a firm theoretical basis, judge whether Mr. Boswell's approach or Monique's approach should yield stronger achievement among the students at St. Procopius.

4. To what extent should Monique be guided by the preferences and observations of the *parents* in the St. Procopius community?
5. If Monique doesn't change her approach, will she be isolated, and will she feel pressure to conform? Should any isolation or pressure influence her thinking?
6. In the end, what should Monique do? Why should she follow the course of action that you recommend?

Related Research and Writing

Select one of the following areas of investigation, research the topic, and produce a brief written report that you can share with your colleagues or classmates.

1. Consult at least one study that reports the effect that direct instruction in grammar has on writing performance. Describe the methodology of the study and summarize the conclusions. To what extent are the results consistent with your own experience? What questions or reservations do you have about the study?
2. Read at least two journal articles in which teachers report their approach to the teaching of grammar. According to the writers, why is there a need and place for instruction in grammar? How do the writers suggest that English teachers should approach instruction in grammar?
3. Examine the approaches to the teaching of written composition that are sponsored by several influential thinkers (e.g., Donald Graves, Lucy McCormick Calkins, Nancie Atwell, Peter Elbow, George Hillocks Jr., Jeffrey D. Wilhelm, Michael W. Smith, Peter Smagorinsky, Thomas M. McCann). According to these commentators, what place does the study of grammar have in the whole English language arts curriculum?
4. Interview at least three English teachers about their experiences with the teaching of grammar. How much do they teach and when do they teach it? How do they teach grammar? After completing your interviews and reflecting on the responses, write your own position statement about the relative importance of the teaching of grammar in the entire scope of an English language arts program. Imagine that this statement would provide a rationale to parents and to supervisors explaining why you teach the way you teach.

16 Teaching English among Many Languages

Preview: Many schools have a population of students who represent a rich tapestry of languages and cultures. At the same time, teachers in most schools follow a curriculum that seems to assume all the students are native English speakers from middle-class homes. While linguistic and cultural diversity brings many advantages to a school, learners who come from homes where English is not the first language can experience many challenges in school. Under these circumstances, teachers must judge how to adapt their practices to meet the immediate needs of a diverse group of learners.

Focus Questions: While the following case has many complications, the narrative prompts two core questions: (1) To what degree is a teacher obliged to follow an adopted curriculum when that curriculum falls short in serving the needs of the learners? (2) How aggressively can a teacher advocate for her students?

The Case: Teaching English among Many Languages

During the first week of the semester, Alysha Buonadonna's informal survey of her third-period English class at Gompers East High School revealed that across the twenty-five students, sixteen speak a language other than English as the first language at home. At the same time, Alysha has observed that almost all of her students speak English fluently when they talk to peers and adults in the hallways and cafeteria. The one exception is Caroline Kaczmerczyk, who recently moved from Poland with her parents, who would not approve her enrollment in an ESL class. Caroline is an eager learner but speaks very little English.

As Alysha got to know her students in this class of eleventh graders, she learned that while some students had very spotty formal education before their families moved to the United States, others had been high-achieving learners in very fine schools. Furthermore, three students have roots in rural areas of the United States, and they speak dialects that are distinct from the dominant dialect of the community.

Alysha's students are enrolled in her English 3 Standard course because they have reading test scores three or more years below their grade placement. The class has a curious profile in that twenty of the twenty-five students identify as boys. A couple of students might have learning disabilities that were never properly identified because limited second language proficiency might have been confused with learning challenges. If this is the case, the students should be receiving additional services by at least having an aide in the classroom. At the other end of the ability spectrum, Alysha judges that three of the girls would probably be in a gifted program if English were their first language. Alysha is tempted to see the assistant principal in charge of registration and sectioning to question the placement of some of her students or lack of support for them, but as a relatively new teacher, she hesitates to come across as a complainer and critic. She is uncertain about how to advocate for these students.

A couple of students might have learning disabilities that were never properly identified because limited second language proficiency might have been confused with learning challenges.

The planning for this class was difficult. Alysha began by following the standard curriculum that a team of teachers had designed many years ago, but she saw right away that students were not responding positively. Basically, they were bored, and many of them struggled with the reading of often anthologized short stories and completing routine activities for learning grammar, usage, and vocabulary. The curriculum guide offered very few opportunities for students to write, as if this were a futile endeavor for students still learning English. When Alysha asked her department chair about diverting from the prepared guide, he cautioned that knowledgeable veteran teachers had planned the curriculum and it should be respected. He observed, "You don't want to coddle these kids by allowing them to avoid difficult materials and tasks. They are very capable if you just make them do what they need to do. You don't want to lower the bar just because these kids come from poor families."

As Alysha labored on with her twenty-five juniors, she became frustrated that several of the students never turned in homework assignments and never completed assigned reading. She worried that with the many missing assignments, students would have a difficult time passing the class; and without having read the assigned texts, students couldn't participate in discussions. Her initial response was exasperation, but as she inquired about the failure to complete assignments, several students shared that they worked several hours a week, which was necessary to contribute to the family income. As she learned more about her students, she discovered that they and their families face a host of financial, health, legal, and housing problems. Recalling the difficult times her

As she learned more about her students, she discovered that they and their families face a host of financial, health, legal, and housing problems.

grandparents experienced when they first arrived from Italy and had to navigate unfamiliar bureaucracies, customs, and practices, even in an Italian enclave in a big city, Alysha could well appreciate the challenges the families of many of her students face. If Alysha's students were to thrive in school, their families would need relief from many serious difficulties. When she shared her concerns with her mom, she said, "You can only do what you can in the classroom. You are not a social worker. You are going to wear yourself out trying to solve all the problems for each family. You have enough to do in teaching English in a responsible way."

Special education teacher Pat Greenway was more sympathetic. She encouraged Alysha to "just be patient with your kids. I know they're not neglecting their schoolwork because they are irresponsible. They need time to learn, especially in reading and writing, and their families need time to resolve some of their problems. They just need your kindness and patience."

But kindness and patience somehow don't seem to be enough. Alysha judges that she will have to do something radically different in the classroom. She appreciates the idea that she needs to teach in a culturally responsive way, but she staggers under the prospect of trying to learn about multiple cultures. A college friend, however, suggested that being "culturally responsive" doesn't mean learning every language and the history of every country of origin, but rather discovering what her students care about and worry about and how they view the world. This friend, Byron Carnivale, encouraged Alysha to be subversive by abandoning the standard curriculum and moving toward reading, discussing, and writing about the issues that most appeal to her learners. She can discover students' interests and concerns by talking to them or asking them to write in response to a related prompt. In Byron's vision, the students will invest themselves in reading articles and perhaps stories about critical issues, such as immigration, marriage equality, gun violence, sexual harassment and sexual assault, equity, and personal liberty. Certainly there is a wealth of materials—including films, music, literature, and news articles—available online, and Alysha could organize the readings, discussions, and writing in a scaffolded way so that she gradually adds to the complexity of the

A college friend, however, suggested that being "culturally responsive" doesn't mean learning every language and the history of every country of origin, but rather discovering what her students care about and worry about and how they view the world.

texts and the nuances of the problems. Alysha can see that such a move would be far more engaging for her students and would be more likely to advance their learning and confidence.

Alysha's hesitation is that in moving in the direction Byron described, she will have to ignore the curriculum that her department chair has encouraged. She might look defiant and perhaps a bit radical, but she feels a keen obligation to serve her students in a way that diverges from the standard curriculum. She also wonders how she can advocate for the proper placement of some of her students and how to lobby for special services.

Questions for Discussion

1. Should Alysha diverge from the standard curriculum to engage English language learners in a more inquiry-based and flexible curriculum? What rationale can you offer to support your recommendation?
2. If Alysha hopes to diverge from the standard curriculum, should she seek the department chair's approval first? How can she defend acting without approval?
3. To what extent should—and can—Alysha involve herself in trying to ease some of the problems that some of the families of her students face?
4. How aggressive should Alysha be in seeking changes for her students' placement and advocating for further support for her students?

Related Research and Writing

Research one of the following topics and share your findings with your classmates or colleagues.

1. Perhaps the teacher in this case would be in a better position to advocate for a change in the curriculum and for support for her students if she could cite the work of influential teachers and researchers who know well the needs of English language learners. Consult the work of at least one of these authorities and compare their suggestions to the practices that you and your classmates or colleagues had judged to be the best. Here are some noteworthy thinkers to consult: Sonia Nieto, David E. Freeman, Yvonne S. Freeman, Carmen Zuñiga-Dunlap, Yolanda N. Padrón, Hersh C. Waxman, and Hector H. Rivera.
2. Interview two or three teachers who work with many English language learners. Prepare a set of interview questions to reveal how they view their

tasks as English teachers and to discover how they think of teaching in a culturally responsive way. To what extent do these teachers see the advocacy for their students as a core responsibility of their jobs? Be prepared to write about your discoveries to share with classmates or colleagues.

3. In the "Teaching English among Many Languages" case, the teacher faces some difficult choices about the curriculum and her role as a teacher. In a brief essay for a reader unfamiliar with the case, summarize and evaluate the possible directions the teacher could take and argue for a particular course of action that you judge will offer the students and the teacher the greatest benefit and the fewest disadvantages.

17

Teaching in the Aftermath of Trauma

Preview: How can we support students' learning when they are experiencing trauma? This case asks the reader to consider when, what, and how to teach when students face collective or individual stressors of the most overwhelming kind. In the following scenario, a second-year teacher grapples with communicating tragic news to students about a fellow classmate and begins to imagine teaching in the aftermath of multiple traumas. The teacher must prepare for seeing students on Monday and decide how to approach the planned curriculum in a time of compounded communal loss.

Focus Questions: (1) When should the teacher share news with students about their classmate? (2) What planning should the teacher do for meeting with students on Monday? (3) How should the teacher treat the students, the curriculum, and the situation in the days ahead?

The Case: Teaching in the Aftermath of Trauma

"omg miss did you hear???!!"

"I'm freaking out rn"

"Is it true? Did he drown?"

Corina Clark's text alerts pinged in her ear. She was out for a run through the park early Sunday evening when her music was interrupted by an influx of messages. Corina stopped along the gravel path to check her phone: several of her ninth graders had suddenly reached out through their class messaging app. They were panicked. Clearly something had happened, but she didn't know what. Before responding to anyone, Corina texted Shanell Anderson, her best friend and fellow teacher at the town's one high school.

"Some of my kids just messaged me and they're upset. Do you know what's going on?"

The reply bubble popped up for a few seconds. Then stopped for longer. Corina had a sinking feeling. She slowly turned around to face the other direction on the trail and head home. Another ping in her ear.

The message on her screen read: "Selvin had an accident last night. He's in the hospital and they're saying he might not make it. Javier messaged me. Something about swimming and a coma."

Selvin was in Corina's second-period class, and Selvin's older brother, Javier, was in Shanell's senior creative writing class. Corina felt her chest tighten. "He might not make it," she said aloud. "How would we go on?" Her small class was very close, and she knew Shanell was in a similar position with her seniors.

She texted back to Shanell, "What does this mean for Monday?"

Corina walked along the curve of the trail, imagining Selvin in a hospital bed, connected to machines with tubes and wires all over his body. She slowed and blinked back tears. Selvin and his family had already been through so much. When he arrived at the start of the school year, he and his brother and dad had just been relocated to the area from the migrant detention facility the next state over. They had escaped violence in Guatemala and sought the perceived freedoms of the United States. The journey from Guatemala was grueling, and they struggled to acclimate once they were able to enter the U.S. Shanell had told her last month that the brothers' dad met with her and shared some of the nightmarish experiences they had had along the way. Now she assumed Selvin was on life support.

Corina walked along the curve of the trail, imagining Selvin in a hospital bed, connected to machines with tubes and wires all over his body.

Last year, her first year at Fern Ridge High School, had begun with news that the beloved assistant principal had succumbed to cancer over the summer. At the start of second semester that year, a sophomore tennis player died from suicide; and right before spring break, she and her then ninth graders were jammed into the corner of the classroom for a terrifying three hours because someone found a gun in a locker. As if those events weren't enough to endure, just before final exams a tornado leveled the south end of town, leaving some in the community homeless, including students. Everyone seemed fatigued from grief. Even their one school counselor looked distraught during the large support groups held for students and staff in the gym.

After each subsequent stressor, Corina did what she thought was right: she invited students to share their feelings, she suggested they write in their class journals, she found links between the texts they were reading and their specific traumas so her curriculum could be responsive to students' needs. Then there came a point after each event when Corina would suggest they needed to move on. Some students would express relief while others lashed out. One eventually stopped coming to class entirely.

Halfway through her second year at Fern Ridge, Corina was now facing the potential for another devastating blow to her class, the school, and community. "It's all too much," she thought.

Corina did what she thought was right: she invited students to share their feelings, she suggested they write in their class journals, she found links between the texts they were reading and their specific traumas so her curriculum could be responsive to students' needs.

She paused to text Marcus Higgins, her district-assigned mentor and the middle school literacy specialist. He'd surely have comforting words and wise advice. "Do you know what happened to Selvin? My students are upset and asking. I don't think we can bear another tragedy."

Marcus responded immediately, "Yes. There was an accident. I'm afraid we should prepare for the worst. Don't say anything to your students yet—we don't have all the information and we need to respect the family's privacy."

Corina texted back, "But they want to know about their friend. They're afraid. If Selvin is hurt, how can I expect them to learn anything on Monday? I was going to introduce the memoir unit you helped me with. It all seems trivial when we're navigating so much right now."

His reply was short: "Keep going with the curriculum. Students need normalcy and routine. We have to stay positive."

Just then another text from Shanell came in. "I think that whatever happens, we need to be honest with our kids. We're always going on about authenticity and preparing for the 'real world.' We ditch our plans and teach to heal. Javier is going to need our support. Being fully present with him and our learning community is critical right now."

They were begging her to respond, to tell them what was happening, to explain what to do.

At that moment, more student messages lit up Corina's phone screen. They were begging her to respond, to tell them what was happening, to explain what to do. She swiped over to her school email account. It was a weekend, but the administration would have to tell the teachers about Selvin, Corina thought. The first sentence of an urgent notice from her principal was waiting for her: "Dear Fern Ridge Community, It is with profound sadness that I share news of . . ."

If you were in Corina Clark's position, what would you do? What would you do if your students were asking for information and your guidance about a potentially tragic situation? What would you do in preparation for tomorrow's teaching? What resources might be available to aid you in supporting your students, your colleagues, or yourself in this time of ongoing trauma?

Questions for Discussion

1. Should Corina respond to her students' messages via the class app or wait until Monday? Would it be better for the news to come from her, the administrators, or others?
2. If Corina shares news about Selvin with her students, how much should she reveal? What are the benefits of students knowing all the details? What are the drawbacks?
3. Is there merit to Marcus's comment that students need "normalcy and routine," and that she should "stay positive"? Why or why not?
4. Is there merit to Shanell's comment to Corina about the "real world" and "teaching to heal"? Why or why not?
5. What do you expect will occur in Corina's classes on Monday? What do you think the students want?
6. What modifications, if any, might Corina make to her plans for instruction moving ahead?
7. To what extent would it benefit Corina to include others in her class meeting on Monday? Who would she involve, and why?
8. What would you recommend as Corina plans for the next twenty-four hours?
9. How can Corina prepare herself mentally and emotionally for tomorrow? How can she prepare her students for the days, weeks, and months ahead through curricular and noncurricular steps?
10. How might these traumatic events inspire new or better policies at Corina's school or the district level?

Related Research and Writing

Research one of the following topics and share your findings with your classmates or colleagues.

1. Consult publications by the National Council of Teachers of English on teaching through trauma. What are some research-supported methods for guiding students through trauma in the English classroom?
2. Talk to a counselor or social worker at your school. What have been their experiences with supporting students, teachers, and schools in times of trauma? How did they respond in the moment and over time? Where are

opportunities for learning from their experiences to prepare for the inevitable moments of trauma in your future as a teacher?

3. Read two articles on the topic of trauma and its effects on learners and educators. How can teachers care for themselves emotionally and physically in times of trauma? How can a teacher who is navigating through emotional episodes appropriately serve learners? What are some strategies for creating compassionate boundaries between the needs of the teacher and those of the students?

18

Can't They Already Read?

Preview: Casual observers might assume that all students in high school can read, at least in the most basic sense of that word. But anyone who has worked in a high school for a time recognizes that despite the best efforts of teachers in elementary and middle schools, some students in high school struggle with reading. It's also true that students *continue* to learn to read in high school, as they encounter increasingly complex texts across disciplines. If the assumption that all high school students can already read is true, teachers could simply assign texts to be read. However, when students need help with reading, assigning them more reading tasks just underscores that these learners are not competent at something everyone in the school seems to value. How can a high school teacher *teach* reading in a principled way?

Focus Questions: The following questions can guide your reading and prepare you to discuss the case with peers or colleagues: (1) How should the teacher approach the teaching of reading with students in high school? (2) What are the choices offered by other teachers, and to what extent does each approach have instructional merit?

The Case: Can't They Already Read?

When Anders Pearson told his mom, a former elementary school teacher, that he was assigned to teach a reading course called Reading for All Occasions to high school students during the new semester, she asked, "Can't they already read? They should be able to read by the time they reach high school. What have they been doing in school for eight or nine years?" Anders explained that many students, for a variety of reasons, still have trouble reading, at least at a high school level. He was in a quandary about how to plan, since he had prepared to become an *English teacher*, not a *reading teacher* in the way his mom had been a teacher of reading for third graders.

Anders judged that it would not be appropriate to try to use his mom's elementary school methods with ninth and tenth graders. Teaching phonics and sight words and reading simple stories together was likely to incite mutiny. His mom offered this advice: "Kids are going to learn to read by reading, so you have to find some texts that will be interesting to them. The formula is *easy reading* and *high interest*, without making the books seem like baby stuff."

Anders judged that it would not be appropriate to try to use his mom's elementary school methods with ninth and tenth graders.

Anders's mom offered some sound advice, as always, but he wasn't sure how he could select texts that would interest all of his students and still be relatively easy to read. You could generalize about the interest of adolescents, but they all had distinct enthusiasms, and some didn't seem to be interested in anything. He recalled a colleague claiming that instead of the teacher picking the reading for students, the learners themselves should select the texts they wanted to read. This would involve accumulating a classroom library of texts so that within the whole collection, there would be something for everyone. But to operate this way would be a radical departure from the way Anders usually taught. Students would have a lot of autonomy, and he would have to rely on something like reading logs to assess that students were reading. This seemed a bit dubious, and his vision of a classroom inhabited by a couple of dozen independent readers contrasted with Anders's usual sense of an interactive learning community.

Anders anticipated what his veteran colleague, Vivian Hirsch, would tell him. Vivian liked to complain bitterly that students couldn't read well because no one *makes* them read. She would prescribe that all students follow the same curriculum, with "time-tested texts" at the core. According to this experienced teacher, English teachers have to assign students to read literature and quiz them to prompt them to complete the assignments. The teacher could model for the students how to read complex literary works, and kids would have to face the consequences if they didn't follow the teacher's example and keep up with their assignments. According to this seasoned veteran, when schools allow students to avoid important literary texts, they are undermining the shared cultural tradition that is part of a humanities education. Anders liked the noble sound of such an effort, but

According to this experienced teacher, English teachers have to assign students to read literature and quiz them to prompt them to complete the assignments.

Maribeth had been teaching the reading course for ten years and had developed a routine that involved the shared reading of some high-interest texts and an independent reading component.

he doubted that his students would actually read mature literary texts, even when threatened with quizzes and tests.

It made obvious good sense to Anders to check with Maribeth Goodsen, the teacher who last taught the course. Maribeth had been teaching the reading course for ten years and had developed a routine that involved the shared reading of some high-interest texts and an independent reading component. This was sort of a combination of Anders's mom's ideas and Vivian's advice. Maribeth listed some titles of books that she thought had universal appeal for adolescents. To Anders, they seemed trivial, and he doubted that high school students would truly find them appealing. Maribeth reported candidly that she did not see much growth in reading over the course of the year with the students in Reading for All Occasions, but she trusted that any reading would benefit the learners, and their literacy growth would take time across their years in high school.

Feeling almost desperate, Anders called his friend Lamont, who taught in another school district. Lamont taught a similar class, which at his high school was a supplement to the conventional English class. Students who had lower scores on a standardized reading test had to take the course. Lamont praised the administrators in his school district for investing in the technology and printed materials to deliver a programmed reading experience for selected ninth and tenth graders. This program relied on extensive computer-based assessments that profiled learners and directed them to "leveled readers," based on their Lexile scores. Learners could access online previews for selected texts and then read independently. The students did little writing, which mostly involved recording notes about the directed reading. Lamont reported that the class "almost runs itself."

If he didn't decide soon on his approach, he would be scrambling when the semester began and spending a lot of time copying short texts or posting material for students to access on their tablets.

The chair of the English department alerted Anders that he would have to submit his request for materials within the next week. Although the budget was small for purchasing texts, Anders could acquire some core texts and plan around those. If he didn't decide soon on his approach, he would be scrambling when the semester began and spending a lot of time copying short texts or posting material for students to access on their tablets. But without a solid set of principles for teaching reading to guide the selection, the purchase of materials seemed somewhat random and bordered on irresponsible.

After consulting with several teachers, Anders remained uncertain. In spite of everything he had heard, he still had no examples of a teacher *explicitly teaching* students how to read complex texts. Also, he was temperamentally resistant to programmed learning and isolated independence that would make any sense of genuine classroom community impossible. Faced with the urgency to commit to an approach and order materials, he wondered how he could show students how a mature reader reads complex texts critically and involve them in reading closely the texts they cared about and would want to discuss.

Questions for Discussion

1. To what extent is it the responsibility of every middle school and high school English teacher to *teach* reading? How would you respond to the question, "Can't they already read?"?
2. Anders believes that he needs to teach reading in a way that is distinct from the way his mother taught reading in early grades. How would you describe the distinctions, if you see any?
3. Anders received advice from several experienced teachers. Summarize each approach the teachers advocate and offer your assessment of the likelihood that it would have a strong effect on learners.
4. Anders seems to gravitate toward an instructional approach that will have students interacting often, perhaps by discussing their judgments about shared reading. To what extent is it important that any teacher foster a sense of community in the classroom? Do you agree that Anders needs to protect this principle?
5. In the end, how should Anders proceed generally in placing his order for materials and approaching reading instruction in high school? What instruction and learning principles have guided your decision?

Related Research and Writing

Research one of the following topics and share your findings with your classmates or colleagues.

1. Many reading researchers and classroom teachers have offered specific directions for the teaching of reading to adolescents. Some noteworthy

authorities are Yetta and Kenneth Goodman, P. David Pearson, Thomas Newkirk, Kelly Gallagher, Nancie Atwell, and Jeffrey D. Wilhelm. Select one of these authorities, or someone else of equal stature, and assess the approach this person advocates. This assessment will first require you to summarize the approach and then evaluate the likely efficacy based on some evidence, including personal experience, or on principles of literacy learning.

2. Some reading enthusiasts, such as Michael Smith and Jeff Wilhelm or Stephen Krashen, encourage teachers to allow students to make their own choices about the texts they read, reasoning that in following their own interests, students will read a good deal and develop reading skills through practice. Report the arguments for free choice in the selection of texts, and evaluate the extent to which honoring a student's reading autonomy will foster skills and a learner's commitment to reading.

3. In this case, Anders's friend Lamont relies on a reading program promoted by a popular publisher. Such programs rely on technology and attempt to match learners with leveled texts. Learn about such a program and report about on how it works, its research base, and your assessment of the wisdom in relying on such a program in a middle school or high school.

4. Early career teacher Anders faces several choices, and he has little time to make up his mind. Evaluate the relative merits of each possibility and recommend an approach to high school reading instruction that you judge will, on balance, have the biggest impact on students' reading skills and enthusiasm for reading.

19

Teacher or Technician? Confronting Standardized Instruction

Preview: How should teachers respond when they are expected to use a highly scripted or standardized set of instructional materials but find that they aren't working for their students? In the following case, a second-year teacher is not sure what to do when his desire to create what he believes will be more effective instruction is met with resistance from his instructional team members, who don't want to make changes in the texts and the standardized set of accompanying materials already in place. The teacher must decide whether to deliver the instructional materials he has been given or to break with the team and introduce new materials in his classroom despite the team's opposition.

Focus Questions: As you read the following case, prepare to discuss these questions: (1) How valid are Rashad's concerns about the instruction he is expected to deliver in his classes? (2) What are some possible courses of action that Rashad could take to deal with the needs of his students and the expectations of his colleagues?

The Case: Teacher or Technician? Confronting Standardized Instruction

As he maneuvered his car into the entranceway by the sign announcing "Home of the Kats," Rashad Amari felt a sense of dread about his eleventh-grade English classes at Kennville High School. Rashad didn't have a problem with his students; it was the curriculum for the course, particularly the upcoming unit he would be teaching. A five-teacher team had developed materials for a unit on nonfiction. Unfortunately, the team had developed the unit before Rashad joined the staff, and he had had almost no input in this curriculum.

During his first year at the school, he had some reservations about the unit, especially its lack of coherence and that the readings didn't appeal to students.

A five-teacher team had developed materials for a unit on nonfiction. Unfortunately, the team had developed the unit before Rashad joined the staff, and he had had almost no input in this curriculum.

When the other teachers on the eleventh-grade team didn't seem interested in Rashad's suggestions for adjustments, he decided that for his first year he should try out the materials his team had developed and focus on learning as much as he could from the other team members, who were all veteran teachers. After all, it was only his first year of teaching, and he thought that the best approach would be to teach the unit before making judgments about it. Maybe his concerns were completely unfounded.

After teaching the unit, Rashad presented some ideas to his team that he believed would improve the instruction and student engagement. The team seemed receptive and suggested that next year he could be in charge of making some revisions to the unit. But before the next year began, some of the team members changed, and the new members were adamant about wanting to follow the instruction developed by the previous team. Even as veteran teachers, they said that since they were new to the course they would feel much more confident following the existing unit, at least for this year.

Rashad was profoundly disappointed. The goals of the unit were for students to be able to read and summarize a nonfiction text and argue a position on some aspect of the text. He felt that these were worthwhile goals, so they were not a problem. The problem was the series of texts that had been chosen. They were random nonfiction texts that had little or no relationship to one another. Each text addressed a different topic or subject: The National Palace Museum in Taiwan, self-driving cars, solar panel construction, endangered sea turtles, the history of the euro, and so forth. The students complained to Rashad that the texts were boring and that they "just couldn't get into them." Rashad used the various instructional materials the team had developed and tried everything he could think of to engage his diverse population of students, but most of the time there was little or no interest in the topic and minimal participation in discussions.

Rashad was concerned about how he could generate more student engagement before his next evaluation with the assistant principal.

When Rashad was observed and evaluated by the assistant principal during his first year, this supervisor identified "student engagement and participation in discussion" as an area for improvement. Rashad was concerned about how he could generate more student engagement before his next evaluation with the assistant principal. He sought the advice of his team members, particularly about how he could improve his evaluation by the assistant principal. They joked about the assistant principal, saying that she was "obsessed with student engagement" and mentioned it in everyone's evaluation. They laughed and advised that everyone knows "it's her idiosyncrasy" and not something he should be too concerned about.

Often Maribel used students' answers as a springboard to provide more extended commentary about her reactions to the text and what she found interesting.

One of the team members, Maribel Mason, a veteran teacher widely respected in the school, invited him to observe her class to see how she engaged students in reading and discussing the texts. Rashad was grateful for the opportunity to observe a respected, experienced teacher. After visiting Maribel's class, he had to admit that her class was definitely better disciplined, more respectful, and more cooperative than his. Unlike his students, Maribel's students didn't complain out loud that the texts were boring, nor ask questions like, "Why do we have to read stuff that sucks? What's the point of these worksheets?" However, to Rashad, Maribel's class didn't seem very engaged. She asked questions about the content of the text they were reading, and only a few students participated. The questions were mostly lower level, and the generally brief student responses didn't reflect much if any critical thinking or analysis. Often Maribel used students' answers as a springboard to provide more extended commentary about her reactions to the text and what she found interesting. Sometimes she told anecdotes about her own experiences related to the text, which the class seemed to somewhat enjoy. Students mostly just sat quietly. At the end of class, Maribel was upbeat, expressing clear satisfaction with the way it had gone. "Students were really on task and attentive from bell to bell," she exclaimed. "I'm so proud of them."

He wanted students to be more involved in discussing ideas and relating the texts to their own lives and experiences, not spending most of their class time taking reading quizzes and answering sets of questions heavily scripted by the teacher.

Maribel's class didn't reflect Rashad's conception of a learner-centered classroom that engaged students in active participation, the kind of environment that was encouraged in his university teacher preparation classes. He wanted students to be more involved in discussing ideas and relating the texts to their own lives and experiences, not spending most of their class time taking reading quizzes and answering sets of questions heavily scripted by the teacher. Though Maribel ran her class like a well-oiled machine, Rashad felt that what he had observed was not going to help with his own classes.

In fact, after teaching the unit the first time, Rashad started putting together materials for what he thought would be a better unit. His students were most interested in the article on self-driving cars and actually got into a brief debate about whether self-driving cars would always be too dangerous even with technological improvements. He was planning to focus the revised unit on "Technology: Is It Making Us Better or Worse?" To go with the text on self-driving cars, Rashad found articles on robot teachers and robot anesthesiologists, social media and mental health, the effects of automation on jobs, the use of computers to grade student writing, and MOOCs (massive open online courses) as an alternative to traditional colleges and universities.

Rashad was confident that together the articles would provide students with facts and evidence to support rich, authentic discussion about whether technology is making us better or worse. He thought that in addition to being more likely to engage students, the approach would better prepare them to fulfill the goals and objectives that the teaching team had established. But at the start of the year, when he presented his ideas to the new team of eleventh-grade teachers, they said they would be more comfortable using the existing materials developed by the previous team of teachers, especially since there were so many materials already available—vocabulary lists, study guides, quizzes, graphic organizers, annotation guides, and so forth. Rashad asked whether he could try out the new articles as a pilot project for the team since he would be focused on the same goals and objectives. They discouraged any deviation from a team approach, explaining that it was problematic to have different materials in different classes because "if there are student or parent complaints, it's easier to justify the instruction when all teachers are doing the same thing. Students and parents can be assured that the materials are part of a curriculum that has been vetted and adopted by all the eleventh-grade teachers." Also, they told Rashad, it's fairer when all students have the same instruction no matter which teacher they have. Since they were in a school where teams constructed common assessments and deliberated about the assessment data as a way to gain insight into how to improve instruction, any deviation from the curriculum would undermine this assessment and improvement model.

Since they were in a school where teams constructed common assessments and deliberated about the assessment data as a way to gain insight into how to improve instruction, any deviation from the curriculum would undermine this assessment and improvement model.

As a reaction to his initial hesitation to teach the units as originally designed, Rashad consulted with his friend Jack Finnegan, who taught English at Fairfield High School. Rashad knew Jack as a bright, confident, and progressive teacher and respected his judgment. In a telephone conversation, Jack advised Rashad that his first obligation was to make learning a meaningful and positive experience for the learners. He encouraged Rashad to "do what you have to do to make the readings, discussions, and writing consequential for the kids." "In the end," Jack insisted, "you have to do what is best for your students, whether or not that pleases your colleagues." That seemed easy for Jack to say, since he worked in a school where he had a great deal of autonomy and was not working in curriculum teams.

He recalled her noting that autonomy is a good thing unless you have a teacher making bad decisions.

Rashad also remembered that under similar circumstances when he was a student teacher, his cooperating teacher, Vivian Scofield, reminded him that the team's coordinated effort was in the end the best for the student body as a whole. He recalled her noting that autonomy is a good thing unless you have a teacher making bad decisions. Autonomy is a positive when each decision-maker is a strong teacher. The common curriculum at least guarantees that all students will receive viable instruction according to a team-negotiated design.

Rashad was not sure what to do. He thought perhaps he was being too idealistic and needed to be more attuned to real-world teaching and working cooperatively with his colleagues rather than trying to apply what he had learned at the university, which seemed to be at odds in some ways with the team-mandated curriculum. He didn't have the same problem in his other course, Creative Writing, because he was the only teacher and therefore didn't work on a team. So he thought maybe he should just be content to design instruction that he felt was best for his Creative Writing courses and go along with the team for the eleventh-grade classes. But over half of his day involved teaching the eleventh-grade classes, and he wasn't sure how he could teach the unit on nonfiction again with the same materials that had been such a flop the previous year. Would that really be in the best interest of his students? What would happen if he simply used the new texts in his own classes to try out this new approach? Could the outcome be any worse, he wondered, than repeating a unit that hadn't worked very well? If he were to introduce new material, in a bit of defiance of the team, would he be open about this effort, or would he teach by stealth? **If you were in Rashad's situation, what would you do?**

Questions for Discussion

1. What are the key issues and conflicts Rashad is facing at Kennville High School?
2. How does Rashad's philosophy of teaching and learning differ from that of the other teachers on his eleventh-grade team? What, if anything, do he and the other teachers have in common? What are the strengths and weaknesses of each viewpoint?
3. How does the instruction that Rashad wants to design differ from the instruction the team has developed? How would you determine which, if either, is better?
4. How effective is the mentorship that Rashad as a new teacher receives from his fellow teachers? What alternative approaches could they have taken in working with Rashad?
5. How important is it for all classes within a grade level to read the same texts and experience basically the same instructional activities?
6. What are some of the possible courses of action Rashad could take? What are the strengths and weaknesses of each?
7. What is the best course of action for Rashad? Why do you think this is the best approach for him to take?
8. For a specific course or at a particular grade level, to what extent should the instruction in different teachers' classes be similar or standardized? Is the ideal situation one in which all teachers are consistently in lockstep or on the same page instructionally? Why or why not?
9. How should teaching teams make decisions about what should be taught and how? How much freedom and autonomy should individual teachers have in designing instruction?
10. What lessons can be learned from this case? For early career teachers? For experienced teachers?

Related Research and Writing

Research one of the following topics, prepare a written report, and share your findings with your colleagues.

1. Interview a veteran teacher or department chair about how curriculum decisions are made in a middle school or high school English department. What experiences has this teacher had with attempts to change a curricu-

lum? What were some of the major problems involved and how did this teacher overcome these problems? What advice does this teacher have for new teachers who want to attempt to change some part of the curriculum in their school? What is your assessment of the teacher's advice?

2. A professional learning community (PLC) is a way to organize teachers into working groups of practice-based professional learning and is used in some schools to promote collaborative learning among colleagues. Read some articles about PLCs in middle and high schools. What are the goals of a PLC? In what ways are teachers typically organized into working groups? What are the benefits of a PLC? Are there drawbacks to organizing teachers in this way?

3. Research information about "developing norms for collaboration" and how engaging in a process of developing norms or expectations for collaboration can help collaborative teams establish an effective working relationship. What is the purpose and value of establishing team norms or expectations for collaboration? What processes or procedures can teams engage in to establish norms for collaboration? To what extent do you think engaging in this process would improve the functioning of collaborative teacher teams? Describe how you would facilitate the process of establishing norms or expectations for collaboration among a team of teachers who are preparing to work together to develop curriculum and instruction.

4. Scripted or standardized curriculum materials are instructional materials, often prepared commercially or by a state or local education organization, that require the teacher to strictly follow a script while delivering lessons. Read a few articles and/or blog posts from professional websites about scripted and/or standardized curricula. What do you see as the value of scripted or standardized instructional materials in an English language arts classroom? What problems might result from a teacher using scripted or standardized materials?

20

Isn't This Getting "Too Political"?

Preview: What should teachers do when they strive to make literature engaging and relevant to their students' lives by relating it to current issues and events but encounter colleagues, supervisors, administrators, or community members who admonish them to avoid controversy and anything that is "too political"? In the following case, a first-year teacher struggles with this question. She has to determine a course of action to take when a colleague worries that the unit she is planning is too political.

Focus Questions: As you read the following case, prepare to discuss these questions: (1) What are the differences in the way the first-year teacher in this case and her mentor are planning to teach the novel *To Kill a Mockingbird*? (2) What differences are there in the advice the teacher is given by various colleagues and family members? (3) What are the benefits and drawbacks of each of the courses of action the teacher considers pursuing?

The Case: Isn't This Getting "Too Political"?

Emma Hemingway is in her first year of teaching at Big Boulder High School, a large high school in a midsized midwestern city. The instructional team for ninth-grade English has decided they will teach Harper Lee's *To Kill a Mockingbird* during second semester, a novel that has been taught for many years in ninth grade at Big Boulder. Emma spent many hours during the winter holidays preparing instruction for the novel. She vaguely remembered reading the novel in middle school or high school, but as she reread it in preparation for teaching, she was captivated by the characters and the descriptions of the small southern town of Maycomb, Alabama, in the 1930s.

In researching the novel, she found a number of current articles and blog posts by respected writers and literary critics that were critical of the novel. She was surprised and curious to discover reasons for the criticism of what she considered a masterpiece of American literature. A number of criticisms focused on the character of Atticus Finch, whom she had initially considered a great father and a social justice hero for his defense of an African American man falsely accused of raping a white woman. One particularly persuasive article criticized Atticus, who is also a state legislator, for being too much of an incrementalist in the struggle against oppression and for not pushing hard enough for significant changes that would bring greater rights and equality to African Americans. Another article argued that we should stop pretending that *To Kill a Mockingbird* is progressive on race and recognize that the novel is criticized for its stance concerning mental disabilities, addiction, the Ku Klux Klan, and the social hierarchy.

Emma also encountered criticism of the extolling of Atticus Finch, an attorney sworn to uphold the law who ultimately agrees to a cover-up of the truth by lying to Maycomb citizens about Boo Radley's role in the death of Bob Ewell. Still another article criticized the novel as a "white savior narrative" and explored the problems of reading a novel about racism in America written by a white author with a white man as the hero, rather than reading one of the many excellent and more authentic novels about racism by African American writers.

After reading a number of articles, Emma wished she could perhaps teach a different novel than *To Kill a Mockingbird*. But she realized that her team was already planning to teach the novel after the winter holidays, and that as a first-year teacher, she would be expected to abide by that decision. So she decided to have her classes read some of the articles that were critical of the novel but balance them out with articles that defended and/or praised the novel. She thought it would be interesting to have her students discuss the different viewpoints and the possible benefits and harms of reading the novel in middle and high schools. Ultimately, her students would be discussing and then writing about whether the novel is a good choice to include as a class novel in middle school and/or high school.

She thought it would be interesting to have her students discuss the different viewpoints and the possible benefits and harms of reading the novel in middle and high schools.

Over the holiday break, as Emma worked on lesson plans for the novel, she became increasingly excited about the value of having her classes explore a real and current controversy about *To Kill a Mockingbird* and to engage in authentic, dialogic discussion. She was convinced that exploring controversies about the novel would work well with the diversity of students at Big Boulder High School, which was approximately 55 percent White, 20 percent Latinx, 10 percent African American, 10 percent Asian, 1 percent Native American, and 4 percent "other." During the first semester, she had frequently been disappointed with the low level of student engagement. Students were often quiet and had little to say when she tried to hold class discussions. She was convinced that her plans for *To Kill a Mockingbird* would turn things around and be more engaging.

When she returned to school after the holidays, Emma couldn't wait to talk with some of her colleagues about her plans. She first shared her ideas with Martha McFee, a veteran English teacher and Emma's mentor in the department. Martha seemed a little distressed as Emma described her ideas for the novel. Martha responded by reminding Emma, "You know we were warned in the fall that we shouldn't be bringing anything political into the classroom. I think you will run into problems with this all being seen as controversial and political. You could easily get some parent complaints about bringing up some of these racially charged issues." When Emma confided that she was really concerned about getting students engaged with the novel, Martha explained that she focuses on the theme of "coming of age" and especially on Scout and Jem, which she considers a much more appropriate focus for ninth grade than "volatile issues about race and white privilege." "I think you will find that ninth graders are not mature enough to deal respectfully and sensitively with the issues you are looking at. You could end up with lots of conflict and division among the students," Martha advised. "You need to play it safe so you don't risk losing your position here."

"I think you will run into problems with this all being seen as controversial and political."

Emma was disappointed in her conversation with Martha. After reading the various articles, Emma felt it would be a disservice to her students and perhaps even detrimental to their understanding of the complex issues related to racism if she approached the novel by focusing on it merely as a coming-of-age narrative and ignored the critical issues that have been raised about the novel. She decided to talk with Samuel Sizer, another beginning teacher in the department. Samuel assured Emma that her plans sounded interesting and motivating for students. He said he hadn't really liked reading the novel when he was in high school, but he would definitely have been interested in participating in the kinds of discussions she described, so he thought her students would be too. However, Samuel advised that maybe Emma should talk to the department chair to get her permission before going ahead with her plans. "In my view," Samuel explained, "it isn't inappropriate or 'too political,' because you aren't talking about particular candidates for political office or specific elected officials, politicians, or political parties."

Emma was conflicted about talking with her department chair because, as Martha McFee had reminded her, it was the chair who at the start of the year had admonished the teachers not to get "political" in the classroom. She had never before asked her department chair to approve her lesson plans, nor was she aware of any other teachers doing so. She was afraid that simply by virtue of asking whether her plans are acceptable she could unintentionally raise a red flag and plant the idea that they are political or controversial.

She had never before asked her department chair to approve her lesson plans, nor was she aware of any other teachers doing so.

Every day Emma was becoming more convinced that the unit would promote student interest, engagement in discussions, and strong, authentic writing. She didn't want to risk having the department chair tell her not to do the lessons she had planned. She also realized that she wasn't even sure what "not being political" or controversial actually meant, or how it was possible to make instruction relevant to students' lives and not be political in some way. She imagined that chances were good that if she taught the novel as she had planned, everything would be fine, but she also worried that perhaps she was being naïve.

Before making a final decision, Emma decided to talk with her father, a science teacher in a neighboring state. After she explained the situation, he said he was impressed by how much thought and work she had put into her planning. He advised that she should do what she had planned but maybe avoid talking with other teachers about what she is doing—"Just close your classroom door and do what you think is best for your students." He also left her with something else to ponder: "Isn't making a choice *not* to share critiques of how issues of race are addressed in the novel a political statement as well?" **Now Emma has to make a decision; what should she do?**

Questions for Discussion

1. How would you evaluate the planning Emma has done for teaching *To Kill a Mockingbird* and her ideas for teaching the novel?
2. How appropriate is the advice that Martha McFee offers as a mentor? Are there other ways she could or should have handled the situation?
3. What different advice does Emma receive about possible courses of action to take? What are the potential benefits and drawbacks of following each person's advice?
4. Is Emma justified in teaching the novel as she has planned? Why or why not?

5. What do you think people mean when they say not to address anything political in the classroom, to leave politics out of the classroom, or to teach in a way that is neutral? Should teachers avoid issues that are political or controversial? Is it *possible* to avoid issues that are political or controversial in teaching ELA?
6. Where should teachers draw the line in terms of appropriate versus inappropriate discussion of what might be called political or controversial issues?
7. What should Emma do in teaching *To Kill a Mockingbird* this time? What would you recommend that she implement as a long-term plan as she continues her teaching career at Big Boulder High School?

Related Research and Writing

Research one of the following topics, prepare a written report, and share your findings with your colleagues.

1. Read some articles in professional journals or blogs that present different viewpoints about whether middle and high school teachers of English language arts can and/or should avoid political issues and remain "neutral" while teaching. Make a presentation to your colleagues or classmates that examines different perspectives on this issue.
2. Interview a few middle or high school teachers about whether and/or how they deal with controversial issues in the classroom. Ask them to talk about specific controversial issues they have either addressed or avoided in the classroom and what led them to make the decisions they made. Share your findings with your colleagues or classmates.
3. Do some research on sources that suggest ways teachers can or should approach controversial topics in the classroom in order to create positive pedagogical opportunities for students. Based on your research, develop a set of guidelines for teachers to help them address controversial topics and issues in the classroom and share it with your colleagues or classmates.
4. Sources abound that provide lists of "Frequently Challenged Books." Select a frequently challenged book that is commonly taught in middle or high school and examine the reasons it has been challenged. Also, see if you can find responses that counter the challenges and objections or that provide rationales for teaching the book, such as those developed by the American Library Association and the National Council of Teachers of English.

III

Reflecting on Practice

Working with Cases: How to Plan, What to Expect

If discussions of case studies are not part of your usual classroom repertoire, you might wonder how the work with the cases is likely to proceed. In our introductory chapter, we suggest some procedures for preparing for discussion of the cases and for inviting written reflections. In this chapter, we offer examples of in-class and online discussion to help you anticipate what to expect and how to troubleshoot when responses don't go quite as expected. We also share an example of a written response that follows discussions.

We also know from experience that instructors and students alike can think of new cases and variations on some of the cases in this collection and might like to construct their own case. Therefore, we offer some general guidelines for writing your own cases.

In-Class Discussion

As with almost any classroom discussion, teachers can imagine a variety of structures and protocols for proceeding. We suggest here some general guidelines that a facilitator might need to adapt for a particular group in a particular instructional context.

- First, we know that discussions are not very productive if students have not had sufficient time to prepare for them. So we suggest that a teacher preview the case and identify the central questions for analysis and discussion. We have built such previews and guiding questions into the introduction to each case. It also helps if students can write down some thoughts about the case before they talk with their peers. In some cases, a teacher might have students work in pairs or other small groups to share their initial impressions about the case. These small-group exchanges prepare participants for the larger conversation in which the class evaluates and compares several recommendations.

- We hold as a guiding principle that if students are expected to write an analysis of a case after they have discussed it, then the exchanges, or intellectual moves, during the discussion should immerse participants in the same procedures that writers will need to command in writing about the case. In practical application, then, the teacher should prompt participants to exercise the same procedures they would in writing: begin with a summary to frame the problem, identify possible courses of action and their likely benefits and possible disadvantages, and show how, on balance, one course of action is preferable to the other possibilities. So, in prompting discussion, the teacher should ask someone to summarize the case. We suggest a protocol by which each participant paraphrases and evaluates the contribution of a previous speaker (i.e., practices *uptake* and *scaffolding*).
- In inviting a full analysis, the teacher asks contributors to identify the possible advantages and disadvantages that could result from a proposed action. The facilitator, then, is not seeking a correct answer for the case, but rather an analysis that attends to the likely outcomes for any proposed action and comparisons among options.
- At some point, after several contributions, the teacher/facilitator will want to summarize the proposed actions and note the potential and the limitations of each. The summary should lead participants to decide which course of action, on balance, offers the greatest benefits and the fewest disadvantages.

For illustration, we focus here on case #18, "Can't They Already Read?" You will recall that the case introduces a high school teacher who is assigned to teach a reading class for which he feels woefully unprepared. We offer excerpts from both a conventional classroom discussion and an online discussion. The classroom discussion is actually a composite from several classes. The excerpt from an online forum is simply cut and pasted as it appeared. We judge that the two examples illustrate what to expect in a typical forum about any one of the cases.

Discussing the Case in the Classroom

For the conventional classroom discussion, the teacher began by asking one member of the class to summarize the situation represented in the narrative. This summary focuses the discussion and initiates the conversation. After the initial summary, the teacher invites clarification or additions. Then the conversation turns to the central question about what the teacher should do.

TOM: Thank you, Sofia, for that summary of the case. Does anyone want to add anything?

LETTI: I agree with what she said. Sofia reported essentially what the case is about. The only thing I would add, though, is that the teacher is under some pressure to submit orders for materials for the next year, so he has to make a choice in a hurry.

TOM: Yeah, so there is a little drama built into the case. So, what could Anders do in this situation? And isn't his mom right—that kids should already know how to read by the time they reach high school?

EMILIA: She's right that all kids can read to a certain extent. I mean, there is something terribly wrong if a student reaches high school and they can't read at all. But I know from my clinical observations that some kids in high school are way behind, like reading at a fourth-grade level, and other kids can read college material. So there are a lot of students who need help to become better readers.

ANTHONY: In high school, you are not, like, teaching phonics and word recognition. I agree with his mom that if kids can just read a lot, they are bound to become better readers, I mean, the more you read, the more fluent you become as a reader, and you develop some vocabulary. The trick is finding some books that students will want to read.

KEENAN: I agree with Anthony that the key is letting students read what they want to read. I remember that when I was in high school, I was reading this fantasy series and I could never get enough of it. But when it came to reading the stuff that was assigned in English class, it was a struggle to stay interested. So I disagree with Anders's older colleague Vivian. Her idea is to stick with the usual literature and force kids to read it through threats of quizzes and bad grades. That is exactly the wrong way to go about things. Kids won't become better readers, and they might end up hating reading.

SOFIA: But I appreciate that Vivian thought she was doing the right thing to expose students to what she thought were important works of literature. I think that there are ways to make that literature appealing and meaningful to learners. I just think she went about it the wrong way. You don't threaten students with failing grades to get them to read.

LATOYA: I think there has to be some sort of balance. I agree with Keenan that you have to encourage students to read whatever interests them. But what are you going to do in class? You can't just have silent reading every day. There is some value in reading a book together and discussing it. So I think that Anders can find some books that will appeal to the class as a whole and then organize an independent reading part of his class so that kids are reading what they want on their own but also sharing with others some books they have read in common.

Discussion of the cases in this book typically takes forty-five minutes or longer. The brief exchange re-created above reveals some of the benefits of talking about the case. In dismissing some recommended approaches to reading instruction and sponsoring other approaches, the participants are evaluating possibilities based on their understanding of how we develop as readers. By and large, they are drawing from their own experience as learners and their observations from the clinical experiences that are part of teacher preparation. As they respond to some mild challenges, they attempt to draw from their knowledge of reading processes and reading instruction to offer a theoretical foundation to support the course of action they would offer to the teacher.

Discussing the Case Online

Teachers have long found some advantages to online discussions. Certainly such forums can prepare class members for in-class discussions. Online discussions can also serve as extensions of the discussions that begin in class. Some of the more diffident members of the class might feel more comfortable contributing to the online forum. We have found that students often express more extensive and carefully prepared comments in online discussion forums, in contrast to the largely exploratory conversations that take place in class. Nevertheless, as you will see next, students reveal that the comments of their peers influence their thinking, leading to more nuanced analysis. Furthermore, the online forums provide a written record of the comments that a class can revisit time and again and draw from if they compose a more elaborated written response.

Among the many impacts of university classes moving online during the pandemic of spring 2020, students were able to participate in learning activities in an asynchronous way. When the pandemic ruptured the routines of families and complicated work and study schedules, students appreciated the flexibility of being able to discuss asynchronously with their peers, and the advantages of such flexibility should probably inform our decisions about discussion forums in the future.

Another university class discussed the "Can't They Already Read?" case entirely online. Although the students were not directed to respond by writing toward a specific length requirement, the discussion was extensive, with everyone participating and many participants responding to each other. The brief exchange below is representative of the entire discussion thread.

AMORI LOVE: During my clinicals last semester, my cooperating teacher assigned in-class independent reading every Friday. Students were allowed to pick their own text for the coming weeks and were assigned a reading log to fill out and summarize their reading for that day. These reading logs helped students remember their text well enough to present the plot to the class in a book report style. Students were excited to share their thoughts about the text with their peers in whatever format was comfortable for them, whether it be a presentation, a video, or something artistic; it was all up [to] them. Considering all that I believe, I think that Anders Pearson should definitely give students freedom because in my experience in my clinicals and as a high school student in a reading-based course, when there is freedom there is more involvement from students.

I have also seen this go the other way where a teacher has assigned a class text for all students to read and they read aloud in class and finished the chapter for homework if it was not completed in class. Students were excited to read aloud or act out scenes, but there was definitely a fair share of students who were not enthused by that method of class. So, Anders Pearson should share two to three class texts they could read and see if they are interested in them. If not, he should allow the students to pick their own texts. There has to be compromise so that students have freedom, but they are still reading effectively and building analysis skills.

In regard to a high school student's ability to read, yes, of course they can read. But the question remains can they comprehend and analyze what they have read? When a student cannot analyze and ponder what they have read, how will they share their thoughts on a text? To me, that is the whole point of reading: not just to obtain information but to also share and create a dialogue around the text. I do feel that some high school students lack the ability to comprehend and analyze a form of literature, but these skills can be taught to students over time. To start the process, students need to have a freedom in their reading materials so that the enthusiasm is there.

KENYAE MAJORS: I do agree independent reading is something that should be done in the classroom, because I look at it as a way for students to engage in reading that they enjoy, and it can give educators a chance to see what students are interested in. Reading should be something that students discuss; and in order for them to discuss the readings they must be able to comprehend what is being read.

BAYLEY FRANZEN: Independent reading sounds great in theory, but how can it be implemented properly in the classroom? One way to get independent reading implemented is to allow for a certain portion of class, like 23 to 30 minutes, to simply revolve around improving their skills. They can read in the same environment, like the classroom, or the teacher can bring their students to the library. If there are students unsure of their reading interests, or they are resistant to reading, they might become inspired by the array of texts waiting to be read. They might even be lucky that their teacher and some of the librarians might provide reading suggestions to help get them started. Perhaps it could be an option for an in-class assignment. Students are assigned specific pages to get read by the end of class, but they are to accomplish this by collaborating with their peers. Yet, some students might feel more comfortable reading and working independently.

As a teacher, I would provide an approved reading list with a wide variety of choices and reading levels. I would set up a structured plan that has clear learning objectives, such as literary elements like setting, character development, and figurative language. The students would of course receive a written copy of this plan, for them to look back and refer to for clarification when needed. In this plan, they have to look for these specific literary elements, and then find examples within their selected text. Then later, we would reconvene in a group for in-class discussion. Our discussion would include talking about an element, and then they would read aloud a paragraph from their book that they thought best illustrates the literary element.

ELIZA KRAMARZ: Not all students can read as well as teachers would like them to. This is why I believe that reading levels should be assessed prior to reading a difficult text, such as something by Shakespeare. Reading has to be taught. As we have discussed in class and through other assignments, children need to be taught strategies for how to be a good reader.

I don't believe that Anders's mother's formula should be applied to students in high school. Her formula may work for younger students because the students have to learn how to read when they are young, and they will more than likely do this if they enjoy what they read. However, students in later grades need to learn how to be better readers, and they cannot just isolate texts that they don't want to read[, like] a complex text such as something by Shakespeare. This is because these difficult works have been taught for hundreds of years, and they will continue being taught. If we are not teaching these difficult works, we are doing children a disservice even if they are not enjoying it at the moment. I am grateful that I learned how to read Shakespeare when I was in high school because it helped me in my college classes today. I did not like Shakespeare, but I persevered, and now I am very happy that I read it. I believe that most students will hopefully come to this realization as well, especially if they pursue a degree such as English or one that uses English a lot.

Vivian believes that "time-tested texts" [are] at the core. Maribeth combines "shared reading" of some "high interest" texts and an independent reading component. Lamont's class uses "extensive computer-based assessments" that profiled learners and directed them to "leveled readers," based on their Lexile scores. I believe that Vivian's approach would work, but I do believe that she should be having some units where students have freedom to choose what they want to read. Maribeth's idea is essentially the one that I have just summarized earlier. I like Lamont's idea, but I don't like that there is little writing in this class.

I think that it is important to have a sense of community in the classroom because this will be essential in students' lives after high school, in careers or beyond. If students only choose what they want to read, students will not have a community feel because students would all choose different books. What I would suggest is having students pick their own books but then having partners of people that have some of the same interests and would enjoy reading the same book and then discussing it in a literature circle, for example.

MATTHEW WOLKOBER: While there is no one-size-fits-all answer to teaching reading, I agree with Anders's mom about the use of "easy reading, high interest." One of the hardest parts about teaching reading is that in most cases, students will not enjoy reading in the same way that we do. It creates a problem because there's already an innate disinterest, which can be detrimental to their comprehension ability. In Anders's situation, he has students who are not reading at level and struggle with their reading comprehension. Therefore, his approach to teaching needs to instill long-term confidence and/or interest in reading.

I think it would be unwise for him to apply a method similar to Vivian's because her method only works toward short-term goals. Yes, students may read for fear of consequences, but that won't make them interested in reading. Likewise, they are not really reading for comprehension if they are only reading for test/quiz answers. Yes, they understand portions of the book, but that will only be because they know they're being tested on it. Plus, if they do read and still fail the tests and quizzes, that will only succeed in destroying any confidence they have in their reading abilities and create a hatred for reading that can have negative long-term academic effects.

A combination of Maribeth's and Lamont['s approaches] could work really well. By using the Lexile scores of the students, Anders could find a selection of "high-interest" books that might interest that student and have them read independently (maybe even adding a book report presentation at the end of their reading), while also using class time to practice reading with some universal titles that may challenge students/help them improve their reading ability in a structured manner.

While I definitely understand Anders's desire to teach students how to read complex texts, I think he needs to build to that goal. Having observed in three Reading classes this semester, I noticed it is essential to target reading interest/confidence before taking on more complex readings. Students don't even need to like reading, as much as they need to be comfortable reading before they can really begin to understand how to approach complex readings.

AUTUMN SOUTH: This is a complex problem that many teachers may struggle with. Overall, I do see value in having individuals find books that they are interested in within a selection that the teacher provides. This way, the teacher has knowledge of the books that their student is reading and can assist them along the way. While many of us, especially after the elementary school phase, truly believe that all students are able to read well enough to keep up with the recommended texts for schools, that is not always the case. The best way, in my opinion, to grow from this is to model reading. If the students were to each have their own text, then the teacher could take pieces and note the way that they would have read it. There are even charts that the teacher can make out that help students follow key features of the text to find a large conclusion for the events occurring.

The one teacher that I disagreed with the most was Vivian Hirsch, especially the portion about having the students face the consequences of not being able to keep up. This is the exact opposite of differentiation, and a teacher cannot expect every single student to be at the same spot in their reading growth. Their comprehension should be the ultimate goal for reading a text and should be less focused on how fast they are able to keep up with others. Anders's mother has decent ideas, especially when it comes to finding novels or texts that the students find interesting. It is important that the student finds a way to enjoy reading, so that when there comes a time for the reading to be less enjoyable, they are able to focus and retain it.

However, I understand that this can pose a challenge when it comes to how a teacher would facilitate multiple texts that they picked. I do believe there are ways to have multiple texts that follow similar themes. These ideas can even be pushed towards the students having to find evidence towards their book's theme being what it is and compare those events and evidence with other students that are reading other books. It's possible to create community even if each student is not on the same book or texts by sharing their own thoughts and evidence from their own novels. This can even be adjusted into smaller groups, where multiple students can be reading one book but then they each discuss with one another. This way, the teacher can go from group to group to monitor and assess how the students are doing. This could even be a chance for the teacher to provide one-on-one time to teach how they would read certain parts of the novel to assist the students in their own reading abilities.

The Quality of Talk

In the directions for contributing to the discussion forum, we asked students to respond to the central question of the case and to consider the set of ancillary questions. We also asked students to reply to someone else's comments so that we had a discussion thread representing the contributions and reactions that a group would normally experience in a face-to-face conversation in the classroom. We have not felt the need to grade the contributions to the discussion forum nor rely on a complex rubric to assess the quality of the discussion. The excerpt above reveals that students were both eager and reflective in their comments, offering remarks that are relevant, logical, respectful of others, and elaborated. Other instructors might decide they need to promote such qualities by formally setting parameters for the discussion.

As with classroom discussions, we enjoy monitoring the online comments so that we can judge how the posts reveal the "effectiveness" of the prompt for initiating discussion. We also enjoy replying to the comments, and students come to expect timely replies. Our replies often paraphrase the comment to check for understanding, but we also like to pose follow-up questions, just as we would in the classroom. So, if we could offer a tip, it is to reply to comments in a timely way, especially with questions that extend the discussion. Students want to know that you are reading and appreciating their contributions.

We expect the online discussion to go somewhere—to have an effect. In the previous example, we wanted students to evaluate several options for responding to the challenge the central character in the case faces. We look for evidence of the kind of procedures that could transfer to a written response: summarizing the situation to frame a problem, evaluating several possible courses of action, and arguing for a course of action that offers the greatest benefit for everyone involved. So, after a series of exchanges, we might offer a summary of the general trend across the discussion forum—sort of saying, "This is what I think we learned from the discussion." We might insert this summary into the forum itself or send it to students by email and invite reactions or clarifications.

An Elaborated Written Response

Each of the cases in this collection offers suggestions for elaborated written responses. Classroom conversations and online discussion forums are important exploratory exchanges, but there is also value in a more carefully considered and thorough written response that takes into account the many possibilities expressed during discussion.

For each case, we offer a few prompts to allow students choices in a written response. We confess to being generous in our grading of such written responses. In reading students' written analyses, we are obviously not looking for a specific "correct" answer about the direction the teacher should take; instead, we look for evidence that the writer has accurately represented the case, evaluated several options, and offered a reasoned judgment for following a specific course of action. In our feedback, we are likely to affirm the quality of the writer's thinking and perhaps pose some questions about the likely outcomes of or complications from the actions that writer endorses. In other words, our feedback remains conversational as we react as readers or conversation participants and not as evaluators.

In the example below, writer Samantha Panek composed an essay after participating in the online forum. The essay reveals Samantha's attentiveness to the discussion about the case; it synthesizes the complex of elements in the discussion forum into her own logical and cohesive statement about teaching reading in high school.

They Can Read, with Our Help

The case "Can't They Already Read?" focuses on how students are able to read the text on a page and understand it at a surface level. However, many students actually struggle with reading into what a text is saying and digging underneath the surface of it. Teacher Anders Pearson is assigned to teach a reading course called "Reading for All Occasions" to high school students. He asks many people for their thoughts on how he should proceed. The people he consults with include his mother, one of his nameless colleagues, colleague Vivian Hirsch, colleague Maribeth Goodsen, and his friend, Lamont. Many of the colleagues and family that Anders talked to shared similar views on how he should teach the course, but there were also some differing views. Anders considers everything that he is told in order to try and create a curriculum that will be the most beneficial for his students.

The different options for this case are represented by each of the teachers that Anders talks to. The first option is his mother, who is a former elementary school teacher. His mother believes that students at this age should already know how to read since they have been reading for years. She does suggest trying the methods she used to teach reading, which are teaching phonics and sight words along with reading short stories together. His mother also offered him this advice: "Kids are going to learn to read by reading, so you have to find some texts that will be interesting to them. The formula is easy reading and high interest, without making the books seem like baby stuff." Although this would teach reading, this method would seem degrading for high schoolers to partake in. They would feel embarrassed that they would have to practice reading in this sense.

Next is the nameless colleague. The nameless colleague does not say much. All they say is that rather than having the teacher pick out the texts that students read, students should be able to select what they read. In order for this to be an option, Anders would have to begin a classroom library and collect different books that students may be interested in. Anders normally does not give students this much choice and independence and is used to teaching in [an] interactive learning community, so he would have to rely on something like reading logs to assess student reading. However, allowing students to choose what they want to read can increase student interest and motivation for reading.

Vivian Hirsch believes that all students should follow the same curriculum with "time-tested texts" being the core of the curriculum. She believes that students cannot read well because no one makes them read. Teachers would use a read and quiz method. Teachers would also be able to model what this looks like and students would have to face consequences if they do not follow the teacher's example and complete assignments. As a seasoned veteran teacher, Vivian states that by allowing students to avoid important literary texts, they are lacking [the] cultural tradition which is a part of humanities. Although it is understandable why Vivian favors this model, it seems as if students are just being forced and controlled to read. There is no pleasure or enjoyment for students with this method.

The teacher who last taught this course, Maribeth Goodsen, has taught it for the last ten years and has found a routine that shares the concepts of reading high interest texts and involving an independent reading component. This is basically a combination of Anders' mom's and the nameless colleague's methods. Maribeth stated that she did not see much growth from the students in this course over the school year, but she believes that as long as they keep reading texts that interest them that their reading skills will improve over their time in high school.

Lastly, Lamont teaches in another school district but has taught a similar class. At Lamont's school, students who had low scores for standardized reading tests are required to take this course. This course is heavily technology based and utilizes a programmed learning experience for struggling ninth and tenth graders. The program directs them to leveled texts for learners, based on their Lexile scores. Students have access to this online and there is little writing done in the course. If there is writing, it relates to the readings in the course. This is a class that can run itself because of the program. This program seems beneficial because it can cater to every student's reading level, but it also seems like it would be costly and a decent amount of money would have to be invested towards it.

Since Anders needs to make a decision for how he should run his "Reading for All Occasions" course, I believe that he should firstly dismiss Vivian's method of teaching the class. Her method of teaching is very outdated and will not foster student enjoyment, which will lead to affecting how they learn. Lamont's method is ideal, but only if the school district can afford to provide the technology and program for the students. If money is not an issue, then I believe that this would be the best way to go about teaching the course. It would allow for students to get help with what they personally need help with. It is very individually focused, which is the best for struggling students since their needs can be met in ways that will benefit them. If money is an issue, then the best way to go about teaching this class would be Maribeth's method. I believe Maribeth's method would be the best to use if money is an issue because it is a combination of both Anders' mother's and Anders' colleague's ideas, which both share similar aspects. Maribeth believes that students should be able to choose what they want to read and should also be shown a variety of texts that may seem interesting to them. The only aspect of Maribeth's I would change would be to ensure that there is some growth with student reading after taking this class. Allowing students to choose what they want to read is significant when it comes to bettering students as readers, but the teacher should also make sure that students are choosing texts they like that will also improve their reading skills. That way, students are able to enjoy reading and improve themselves as readers simultaneously.

Samantha Panek

Samantha's review and analysis reveal that she has attended to the several contributions of her peers in the online discussion forum. She has gone beyond simply cutting and pasting the posts that she likes; she is able to summarize the views embedded in the case narrative and endorsed or criticized in the discussion forum. Her review leads to her summary evaluation in which she combines approaches and shows how a particular course of action is likely to be most advantageous for learners, thus benefiting the teacher in his search for a principled way to teach reading.

Again, in the written response we are not looking for an endorsement of our preferred method of teaching. If that were the case, we could lecture a class and administer a forced choice test. Instead, we hope to promote procedures for problem solving, especially when the problem-solving process includes consultation with peers and attention to competing perspectives. In the end, we look for evidence of analytical thinking and an expression of a principled approach to the teaching of English language arts.

A Guide to Writing Your Own Cases

Anyone who spends a significant amount of time in schools will recognize tough situations and troubling issues that emerge on almost a daily basis. The cases contained in this book cannot represent all the challenging situations a teacher might face and about which a teacher should be aware. The educational landscape changes constantly (perhaps illustrated most profoundly by the global pandemic of 2020), and every school provides a unique context for teaching. Obviously, the issues represented by the cases in this book are not exhaustive. It would be worthwhile for students and instructors to attempt to write their own cases after working with a few of the cases included in this book. Perhaps discussion will reveal ancillary but important issues, and an instructor or team of students will be inspired to write their own case. Our experience in working with case studies and in facilitating discussions suggests that for any new case to produce meaningful discussion and spark related research, it should have the following features:

1. *Central Problem*: The case should introduce a central problem that readers will find consequential, so the problem should be a significant one. A reader will evaluate the significance by determining how much potential there is for a similar situation to confront any teacher and for the response to the problem to have a substantial impact on the teacher and learners. From the case narrative, the reader can judge how the choices in the case can affect a teacher's career and can have an impact on several players in the drama.
2. *Realistic Narrative*: The situation has to be real. There must be sufficient detail, then, to make it real: Who are the characters? Where does the story take place? Why is there conflict? Where is there dialogue? The reader should recognize the situation sufficiently to acknowledge that such events occur and could visit any teacher.
3. *Invitation for Reader Involvement*: You have to involve the reader. What is the reader's role in the case? Have you put the reader in the place of the central character? Can you help the reader feel a sense of urgency to take some action? What do you want the reader to do?
4. *Some Complications*: The central problem of the case should seem an authentic one through complicating factors that make it difficult to arrive quickly at a simple or obvious answer. The case should represent the idea that choices have consequences and that sometimes obvious choices are blocked by other pressures and circumstances. Most teachers will figure out the easy problems on their own; the complicated problems are the ones that invite consultation with other thinkers.
5. *Multiple Perspectives*: The case should recognize that any group of educators is likely to represent multiple perspectives. Giving attention and respect to many points of view is a good habit of critical thinking. The case will be richer if it includes several voices and recognizes that there may be several legitimate and rational ways to think about the central questions of the conflict.
6. *Specific Procedures*: Describe the procedures you want readers to follow in order to think about, discuss, and write about the case. Readers might recognize that as students they were eager to learn from instructors, "What are we supposed to do?" The case, then, should not baffle the reader about the procedures, but should suggest a process for working with the case and deliberating with others about how to work constructively to resolve the conflicts.

There are abundant sources for case study topics. If someone is already observing or working in a school, it will be fairly simple to recognize sources of difficulty. If you were to return to the middle or high school you attended as a student, former teachers can tell stories about some of the concerns they have had and some of the frustrations they have experienced during their careers. If a group of colleagues or classmates were to produce a set of case studies, a pattern might emerge that could help a new teacher anticipate the major challenges they will face. Discussion about a variety of cases is likely to equip a teacher with the tools to work through some difficulties in order to concentrate on the rewards and positive aspects of a teaching career.

References

Atwell, N. (2014). *In the middle: A lifetime of learning about writing, reading, and adolescents* (3rd ed.). Heinemann.

Calkins, L. M. (1994). *The art of teaching writing* (New ed.). Heinemann.

Cooper, J. M., & McNergney, R. F. (1995). Introduction: The value of cases in teacher education. In J. M. Cooper (Ed.), *Teachers' problem solving: A casebook of award-winning teaching cases* (pp. 1–10). Allyn & Bacon.

Dunlap, D. Z. (2015). *Helping English language learners succeed* (2nd ed.). Shell Education.

Elbow, P. (2007). Reconsiderations: Voice in writing again: embracing contraries. *College English, 70*(2), 168–88.

Freeman, Y. S., Freeman, D. E., with Mercuri, S. (2002). *Closing the achievement gap: How to reach limited-formal-schooling and long-term English learners*. Heinemann.

Gallagher, K. (2009). *Readicide: How schools are killing reading and what you can do about it.* Stenhouse.

Goodman, K. S., & Goodman, Y. M. (1979). Learning to read is natural. In L. B. Resnick & P. A. Weaver (Eds.), *Theory and practice of early reading* (pp. 137–55). Erlbaum.

Graves, D. H. (1983). *Writing: Teachers and children at work.* Heinemann.

Grossman, P. L. (1992). Teaching and learning with cases: Unanswered questions. In J. H. Shulman (Ed.), *Case methods in teacher education* (pp. 235–55). Teachers College Press.

Hillocks, G., Jr. (1995). *Teaching writing as reflective practice.* Teachers College Press.

Hillocks, G., Jr. (2006). *Narrative writing: Learning a new model for teaching*. Heinemann.

Hillocks, G., Jr. (2011). *Teaching argument writing, grades 6–12: Supporting claims with relevant evidence and clear reasoning*. Heinemann.

Johannessen, L. R., Kahn, E. A., & Walter, C. C. (2009). *Writing about literature* (2nd ed., rev. & updt.). National Council of Teachers of English.

Johannessen, L. R., & McCann, T. M. (2002). *In case you teach English: An interactive casebook for prospective and practicing teachers.* Prentice Hall.

Krashen, S. (2011). *Free voluntary reading*. ABC-Clio.

McCann, T. M. (2014). *Transforming talk into text: Argument writing, inquiry, and discussion, grades 6–12*. Teachers College Press.

McCann, T. M. & Kahn, E. A. (June 2017). What are the concerns of beginning English teachers? [Paper presented] English Education Summer Conference, Ohio State University, Columbus.

McCann, T. M., Johannessen, L. R. & Ricca, B. P. (2005). *Supporting beginning English teachers: Research and implications for teacher induction*. National Council of Teachers of English.

McNergney, R. F., Ducharme, E. R., & Ducharme, M. K. (Eds). (1999). *Educating for democracy: Case-method teaching and learning*. Erlbaum.

Merseth, K. K. (1991). *The case for cases in teacher education*. American Association for Higher Education and the American Association of Colleges for Teacher Education.

Newkirk, T. (2011). *The art of slow reading: Six time-honored practices for engagement*. Heinemann.

Nieto, S. (2017). *Language, culture, and teaching: Critical perspectives* (3rd ed.). Routledge.

Padron, Y. N., Waxman, H. C., & Rivera, H. H. (2003). Educating Hispanic students: Obstacles and avenues to improved academic achievement. *ERS Spectrum, 21*(2): 27–39.

Pearson, P. D., & Johnson, D. D. (1978). *Teaching reading comprehension*. Holt, Rinehart and Winston.

Schön, D. A. (1983). *The reflective practitioner: How professionals think in action*. Basic Books.

Smagorinsky, P., Johannessen, L. R., Kahn, E. A., & McCann, T. M. (2010). *The dynamics of writing instruction: A structured process approach for middle and high school*. Heinemann.

Small, R. C. Jr., & Strzepek, J. E. (1988). *A casebook for English teachers: Dilemmas and decisions*. Wadsworth.

Smith, M. W., & Imbrenda, J.-P. (2018). *Developing writers of argument: Tools and rules that sharpen students' reasoning*. Corwin.

Smith, M. W., Wilhelm, J. D., & Fredricksen, J. E. (2012). *Oh, yeah?! Putting argument to work both in school and out*. Heinemann.

Spiro, R. J., Coulson, R. L., Feltovich, P. J., & Anderson, D. K. (1988). Cognitive flexibility theory: Advanced knowledge acquisition in ill-structured domains. In *Tenth annual conference of the cognitive science society proceedings* (pp. 375–83). Erlbaum.

Spiro, R. J., Vispoel, W. L., Schmitz, J. G., Samarapungavan, A., & Boerger, A. E. (1987). Knowledge acquisition for application: Cognitive flexibility and transfer in complex content domains. In B. K. Britton & S. M. Glynn (Eds.), *Executive control processes in reading* (pp. 177–99). Erlbaum.

Sykes, G., & Bird, T. (1992). Teacher education and the case idea. In G. Grant (Ed.), *Review of research in education, 18*. American Educational Research Association.

Wilhelm, J. D., & Smith, M. W., with Fransen, S. (2014). *Reading unbound: Why kids need to read what they want—and why we should let them*. Scholastic.

Related Resources from NCTE

The National Council of Teachers of English (NCTE) provides an abundance of resources for current English language arts teachers and those preparing to become ELA teachers. We have listed a few resources here that we judge to be useful supports for thinking about the cases in this book and for researching related issues and fostering further discussion.

NCTE Quick-Reference Guides

NCTE provides several Quick-Reference Guides: ncte.org/resources/quick-reference-guides/. The following titles link closely with cases offered in this book.

Akhavan, Nancy. *Literacy Instruction for Students Living with Trauma*

Buehler, Jennifer. *Teaching Reading with YA Literature*

Dean, Deborah. *Teaching Grammar in the Secondary Classroom*

Dean, Deborah. *Teaching Secondary Writing*

Smagorinsky, Peter. *Unit Design in the ELA Classroom*

NCTE Intellectual Freedom Center

ncte.org/resources/ncte-intellectual-freedom-center/
NCTE's Intellectual Freedom Center is an especially valuable resource for teachers who face censorship challenges and other forms of resistance against intellectual freedom.

NCTE Position Statements

NCTE provides several position statements that help teachers navigate through instructional challenges and sensitive societal complexities. The following list identifies statements that we judge to be particularly relevant to the cases in this book.

The Act of Reading: Instructional Foundations and Policy Guidelines
ncte.org/statement/the-act-of-reading/

Expanding Opportunities: Academic Success for Culturally and Linguistically Diverse Students
ncte.org/statement/expandingopportun/

NCTE Position Paper on the Role of English Teachers in Educating English Language Learners (ELL).
ncte.org/statement/teaching-english-ells/

Resolution on English Education for Critical Literacy in Politics and Media
ncte.org/statement/resolution-english-education-critical-literacy-politics-media/

Shifting from Professional Development to Professional Learning: Centering Teacher Empowerment
ncte.org/statement/proflearning/

Statement on Academic Freedom (Revised)
ncte.org/statement/academic-freedom-copy/

Statement on Anti-Racism to Support Teaching and Learning
ncte.org/statement/antiracisminteaching/

Understanding and Teaching Writing: Guiding Principles
ncte.org/statement/teachingcomposition/

Index

Authors

Dianne Chambers is a professor of English at Elmhurst University, where she teaches courses in American literature, film studies, women writers, and fiction. She also works closely with students who are training to become English teachers and teaches the methods class for prospective English language arts teachers. She is the author of *Feminist Readings of Edith Wharton*.

Sarah Hochstetler is a professor of English education in the Department of English at Illinois State University. She is a former middle and high school English teacher, current literacy consultant and coach, and National Writing Project fellow. Her writing about teaching and learning has been featured in practitioner-focused publications such as *English Journal* and *Voices from the Middle.* Hochstetler is editor of the book *Reform and Literacy Education: History, Effects, and Advocacy*.

Elizabeth A. Kahn is an associate professor of English at Northern Illinois University. She formerly taught high school English for thirty-six years and served as an English department chair. She is coauthor of *Discussion Pathways to Literacy Learning, The Dynamics of Writing Instruction, Writing about Literature*, and *Talking in Class* and coeditor of *Inquiry Paths to Literacy Learning, Raise Your Voices*, and *Inquiry Units for English Language Arts*.

Thomas M. McCann is a professor of English at Northern Illinois University. He is a former high school English teacher and school and district administrator. His books include *Transforming Talk into Text* and *Literacy and History in Action*. He is the coauthor or coeditor of *Supporting Beginning English Teachers, Talking in Class, Discussion Pathways to Literacy Learning*, and *Raise Your Voices*.

This book was typeset in TheMix and Palatino by Barbara Frazier.

Typefaces used on the cover include Montserrat and Fjalla One.

The book was printed on 50-lb. White Offset paper by Seaway Printing Company, Inc.